The Improvement Engine

The Physics of Success

THEORY AND TOOLS FOR TRUST ENGINEERING

Matt Rollins

authorHOUSE®

AuthorHouse™
1663 Liberty Drive
Bloomington, IN 47403
www.authorhouse.com
Phone: 1-800-839-8640

Published by AuthorHouse 10/03/2017

ISBN: 978-1-4969-0371-6 (sc)
ISBN: 978-1-4969-0372-3 (e)

Library of Congress Control Number: 2014908888

Print information available on the last page.

Any people depicted in stock imagery provided by Thinkstock are models,
and such images are being used for illustrative purposes only.
Certain stock imagery © Thinkstock.

This book is printed on acid-free paper.

Contents

Dedication:

I wanted to take a moment to share my feelings as this book is being published. My name is Sheri Brainard, and I was so lucky to be a trusted friend, confidant, and colleague of Matt Rollins. He and the love of his life, Rose Rollins, mean the world to me. They entrusted me with Matt's gift to the world. What an awesome and precious task . . .

You see, Matt had worked on The Improvement Engine and The Physics of Success for many, many years. Honing it, studying it, learning from it, teaching it, and then ultimately wanting to share it with the world became his passion. He *knew* that he was onto something big! He had cracked the formula for why some people, relationships, and organizations were successful where others were not. This book captures and shares that insight.

Let me tell you a little history. Matt Rollins and I worked together in a number of Fortune 100 companies. He and Rose were married the same year that my husband, Scott and I were. He helped teach my son Ryan how to barbeque at his famous "Pork of July Parties" and even passed on his famous "rub" recipe. They also shared their love for the guitar and singing.

Matt and I shared so many friends and colleagues. We talked through projects, his song writing, philosophy, work results and or failures, family illnesses, relationships and achievements over many meals. We traveled all over the world together. We both intensely loved ours and each other's families. We did life together.

One of my favorite and most memorable nights of my life was in North Carolina at the home of Stan and Shannon Osgood. These two were always so good to invite those of us from out of town/country over to their home for some home cooked meals and generous hospitality. This night was different, though. Matt had finished his final draft of this book, The Improvement Engine. He gave the transcript to a group of us to read and provide feedback. Stan, who worked with Matt and

I, decided it would be nice to have a group of colleagues over with the sole intent to discuss and provide feedback to Matt on his book. There was no music. No TV. Just Matt Rollins, Stan Osgood, Shannon Osgood, Marjorie Hook, John Henry, Dave Olski and myself, food and a few bottles of good wine. We talked for hours. This was the most intellectually stimulating and insightful conversation I can ever remember having. The Improvement Engine gave us the platform to explore our deepest beliefs in leadership, improvements, values, and human behavior. The reason was more than the fact that we had all been intimately involved in improvement and change management around the world. There was something special about this Improvement Engine, trust and learning, and the entire Physics of Success. On the surface, we weren't sure that the book itself, would make it to our top 5, and that concerned us. You see, Matt's message and discovery were powerful, and we wanted his book to reflect this revolution. We knew that it had eluded all of us as to how to create "mini me's" or "mini us's" as it was, when it came to helping corporations help themselves. Companies and their executives always wanted to replicate what those of us who had been in the business, and were seasoned improvement change agents (which really meant were older than dirt!), brought to the table. So, we knew that there was something to the discussion and learning that went on each and every time you discussed The Improvement Engine. Hmmm, this was now a dilemma that Matt and I discussed many times over the next year.

The struggle with how to duplicate and teach the secret of success at the Executive Level became our constant conversation in our travels. The answer became more and more pressing as Matt's cancer returned. He had been battling cancer for a number of years. And, in fact, we both strongly believe that the fact that he and his doctors had a strong and very successful Improvement Engine working between them was what allowed him to defy the odds for so many iterations of this tough disease.

There came a time when we realized that Matt's disease was now terminal. I feel so fortunate that Matt and Rose allowed me to be a part of this last sweet part of their love story. Thank you both from the bottom of my heart.

Matt knew that his message was of equal importance to the world as the works of Deming, Juran, Crosby and other Quality and Leadership Gurus. And, I knew it was too. I believed in him as a man, and I believed and supported his work as a professional. Matt was one of the smartest people I had ever met. He went to college at 14! I mean, who does that! I've only personally known a couple. But, what set Matt apart was his uncanny ability to relate to all levels of an organization in spite of his brilliance! When you met Matt, you met a lifelong friend. Someone you could trust. Someone who would share every bit of knowledge he had. He was also a life learner and pursued knowledge of all kinds. His goal was to demystify tough subjects like statistics, physics, analytics, relationships, and leadership so that others could be better because he had touched their lives. He epitomized a well-oiled Improvement Engine.

So, with the Improvement Engine draft completed and the formulas for the Physics of Success created, and the terminal "verdict", there was an impending deadline for closing the final chapters of Matt's lifelong work. He and I spent hours upon hours, week after week, month after month, going through each and every word of his manuscript. He wanted to be sure I knew exactly what he meant by each carefully selected word he had written. He wanted me to challenge every thought, every experience, and compare it with what I believed to be true. I became his student, and he mine. He and I continued to learn from each other right up until the very end. One or the other of us would have their beautiful gray cat named "Grady Cat" on our lap. Grady Cat was our constant companion. Even when Matt was in the hospice bed in the living room, he, Grady Cat and I would continue our discussions.

We reached out to Dr. Dennis Romig, the New York Times #1 best-selling author of both books "*Side-by-Side Leadership*" and "*Breakthrough Teamwork*". Dennis graciously agreed to peruse the book and compare it to his research as well as provide editorial insight. A special thank you to Dennis, and his wife Laurie, for their friendship, their work, and their help with this book. Matt and I both respect your work, have enjoyed working with you throughout the years, and appreciate all you have taught us.

After one tough doctor's appointment, it became evident to Matt that he was not going to get to see the day his book was published. He and Rose invited me over for a heart-to-heart talk about this book among other spiritual and relational topics. *Matt asked if I would complete his book and see that it got published.* I was honored and filled with an overwhelming sense of responsibility to do his life's work justice. We immediately sought the adult Make a Wish Foundation to try to make the publication possible while Matt was around to see his dream to fruition. But, that wasn't meant to be. Time was too short. Matt Rollins died peacefully and happy with the love of his life Rose Rollins by his side. He also knew he had documented and left for the world a recipe for success. He was content.

One of the last things Matt told me was that he wanted Rose to be well taken care of, to know how much he loved her, and for her to be proud of him as a man. He also hoped that his Dad, his son, and his niece, were proud of his life's work as documented in the Improvement Engine. He wanted his family and friends to know how much he loved them and how happy they made him.

He hoped his music would live on.

The message he wanted to pass onto his colleagues and all of you in the world of continuous improvement comes with a short story. Every day when he and I would go into a corporation around the globe, before we got out of the car to go in, I'd lead us in a prayer. The prayer always incorporated the following 2 thoughts:

- Lord, please help us to give this company, it's leaders, and it's employees, not only what they want, but what they need.

- And, Lord, please help them to see You through our behavior.

After we concluded the prayer, he would always say "Worse is going to have a bad day!" This simply meant that we intended to leave the place improved. Anything that was bad, or wanted to get worse, was going to really have a bad day!

So, in conclusion, as the 8th anniversary of Matt's death has come and gone, you might wonder why it has taken so long. Well first, I don't know if Rose was ready. Then, I wasn't. You know the grief process is a funny thing.

We wrestled back and forth with whether to change Matt's manuscript to make it unique or put it in story format. Matt knew of all of these options and said he trusted my judgment explicitly. We even talked of weaving a story of his life and his journey with cancer throughout.

But, when all was said and done, we left Matt Rollins' version of the Improvement Engine and the Physics of Success 100% intact! The only iterations were the edits that he and I had agreed would be incorporated from Dr. Dennis Romig's input.

What Rose and I agreed would happen is that I would write a Workbook to accompany Matt's work. This workbook would be intended to be used by a team of leaders over the course of several weeks or months. With this approach, an opportunity for a conversation among leaders is created, much like the dinner meeting that was earlier described. Each leader should read a Chapter of The Improvement Engine. Weekly the entire leadership team shall discuss a specific chapter using the Workbook as a facilitated guide through learning about and enhancing the Improvement Engine that already exists in their organization or lives.

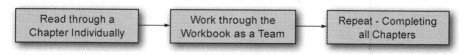

Read through a Chapter Individually → Work through the Workbook as a Team → Repeat - Completing all Chapters

This approach makes The Improvement Engine unique. To my knowledge, there is no other leadership, improvement or quality text that has the "how to" workbook with it. Now when asked if The Improvement Engine will make my Top 5 list, I can honestly answer "YES"!

I look forward to putting The Improvement Engine and The Physics of Success into many organizations in the future. The future where "worse is going to have a bad day"!

Matt, my friend, your dream has now been finished . . .

"In loving memory of Matthew David Rollins, the best person I have known, or ever will know. He was a shining example, to every soul he touched, that life truly is good." Jason Rollins

Matt always said he was the luckiest man in the world to have found me. However, I feel I am the lucky one to have been a part of his life for 20 years. He was always positive and very supportive of my endeavors in work and life. He told me daily that he loved me and knowing that has given me the strength to continue on the journey God has planned for me. Although God's plan for Matt took him away from me, I know he is always with me in spirit. Thank you, Matt for all of the wonderful lessons you shared with me. I am a better person for having you in my life.

Rose Rollins

Foreword

"We know truth, not only by reason, but also by the heart."

Blaise Pascal

You will quickly notice that this foreword has not been written in the traditional third person. The same is true for the entire book, in fact. I do this for two reasons. First, I think that an interaction between you and me is likely to build trust. I propose rather that this book be a conversation between you and me—a bit one-sided, perhaps, but you will find I ask questions of you which have you responding, so though I do not hear it, I plan for and acknowledge your participation. After all, much of what I hope to teach is merely a new viewpoint on your own experience, so your contribution is critical to the book's success.

I am going to assume that you are reading this book in order to learn something. If it is indeed the case that you hope to learn, then it is important that you trust me. That may come as a bit of a surprise, certainly a rather high expectation on the part of any author. However, it is a significant theme of this entire book that learning and trust are interdependent.

Any reader adventurous enough to begin this book deserves to know the pattern of events and thinking that created it. This overview is the foundation of our trust. It is important in building our trust—that my fundamental values are revealed for some examination. As you will see, such understanding and trust are necessary to the working of the

Improvement Engine. It is my first goal to start that Engine working to your benefit. So, in order to help you know me and—hopefully—begin to trust me, I offer you the following short biographical summary and a reference to writings and people that have influenced my own thinking, and development of the Improvement Engine.

Parents obviously have a lot of influence over both what and how a person thinks. My father was an electronics engineer who graduated from MIT and spent the early portion of his career on the edge of one of science's technological and ethical frontiers: atomic testing. My mother was an artist and a storehouse of information from the worlds of art and literature, as well as stories from her family dating back generations before her birth. From both of them I learned to find wonder in a lot of places. For every wonder, I always asked, "Why?" and "How?"—and pursued the answers in a basically scientific manner. (I'm pretty sure that last part was mostly from my dad).

I began my university studies with the thought of becoming a physicist. My exposure to the subject in high school was, thanks to the energies and patience of a truly fine teacher and the help of my father, a key in all my future thinking, for it seemed to me to reduce the complexities of the universe to simple elements: constants and equations, stable in themselves, but malleable in the hands of creative intellect, capable of transforming theory to invention. Mechanics and optics seemed especially charming in their ability to explain themselves in a very few equations, all sensibly bound to each other in a hierarchy that was almost visual in my imagination. I could sense in an almost intuitive, sensual manner how they worked with, played against, and balanced each other.

The same could not be said for calculus, which I encountered in my first year of college. The very concept of limits (you almost get there, but not quite . . . ?) seemed somehow . . . disorderly. My discomfort with the subject was such that I turned to a study quite removed from the solidity and dependability of the physical sciences: English literature. Yet here, too, I discovered that there were certain universal simplicities at play, though they were expressed in more complex ways. From Beowulf to James Joyce we find that writers have perceived the same fears and joys, operating perhaps in different environments, but nonetheless essentially identical at the root. People universally cherish the love of those they themselves hold dear. They fear death, and they fear the dying even more. The simplest of differences can be the greatest of separators. However complex life may grow as time passes and man's imagination fills the world with more and more choices, the most primary issues stay the same, and they have about them the same sort of simple elegance as the laws of light and motion.

By the time I had finished most of a PhD focusing on Shakespeare and the literature of the American West, I came to an interesting nexus of thought, opportunity, and poverty. Academia had come to be a burden of theory with little application; I felt no attachment to a product or end result of my activity. I yearned for a little prosperity and creature comfort. Ultimately, I was offered a job that was to have more meaning than I could ever have expected—as a technical writer of procedural specifications in a semiconductor manufacturing facility (termed "fab" for "fabrication area" by those in the industry). On the surface, this might seem far removed from any goal my education might have presupposed, and, in truth, I took the job just because it seemed like pretty darn good money for something that I was sure I could do.

In retrospect, the mission for that job combined more of what I valued than I knew at the time. Specification writing in the chip-making business amounted to expressing in very simple terms the directions for carrying out one of the most complex and scientifically challenging manufacturing operations in the world. The tools used in the fab were, in many cases, still scientific experiments themselves. The industry applied technology that many research labs would have envied. Yet the people running these tools, and often the people supervising them, often had no more than a high school degree and no particular interest in the sciences. My challenge in writing instructions for these people to do their jobs was twofold. First, I had to accurately and simply explain the procedure for running the tool. Second (and much more difficult), I needed to build into those instructions just enough information for them to be able to understand the consequences of incorrect operation. In pursuit of this end, I found what turned out to be the core activity of my entire professional career: summarizing and synthesizing the complex so that it may be understood simply.

It was the early 1980's. Most of American industry was waking up to a fact that a few industries had discovered in the 1970's: global competition, especially Japanese, was a genuine threat. Overnight, it seemed, a country whose very name was synonymous with cheap, disposable goods was present and competitive in marketplaces where American superiority (or at least advantage) had been assumed for decades. The semiconductor industry, in particular, had just realized that this threat was upon them as they found that Japanese fabs were often getting higher yields and shorter cycle times while using older equipment and maintaining lower inventories than their American counterparts. The Quality Revolution was upon us. Technology provided—and demanded—more data. Computers gave us exponentially more powerful tools to use that data. Information and technology both became globally available. Under such conditions, the pace of improvement, and therefore the pressure of competition, were bound to increase.

It was in this period that I discovered two of what have come to be the four main external inputs to my thinking. The first was the phrase "continuous improvement." I remember to this day the rush of discovery that filled me the first time I read that phrase and realized all that it implied. Even as a relative novice to the world of industry, I could see that the term introduced a revolution in thinking, a departure as abrupt and significant from what had come before as Arthur C. Clarke's black monolith in the world of the ape men from <u>2001: A Space Odyssey</u>. Today, of course, the term has been used, overused, and even abused to the point that, like many clichés, it has lost meaning. Back then, though, many people were still seeing and hearing that phrase for the first time, and the impact was tremendous.

(By the way, I have made my first reference to another author. To the horror, I'm sure, of my college professors, I have not done standard footnoting in this book except in Chapter 7, where I reference particular studies that make specific points. In all other cases, I have simply referred to the work of the author. For a complete list of the works referenced in this book, see the "References and Notes" section at the end. It also includes my own comments on the content of each work referenced.)

The second input I discovered in researching the first. It does not take long in reading about continuous improvement to run across the name of Dr. W. Edwards Deming. By expressing the impact of Deming on my thinking, I do not in any way mean to detract from many others who articulated and led the Quality Revolution. Shewhart, Ishikawa, Juran, Crosby, Taguchi, and others are key contributors to the knowledge that enabled the Quality Revolution. William Ouchi's <u>Theory Z</u> brought discussions to both boardrooms and cafeteria lunch tables that ended up shaking the foundations of management. Deming, though . . . well, Deming just sang to me. The importance of correctly analyzed data, the cost of poor quality, the fallacy of exhortations to productivity, and the responsibility of management all came together, under Deming's relentless logic and anecdotal evidence, as a philosophy that could not be ignored, and whose only conflicting argument was the pathetically impotent "that's not the way we do things here." I think that his irreverence for management—his quite palpable impatience for those in leadership positions who didn't "get" what he was saying—was part of what engaged me.

By 1983 I knew that the pursuit of continuous improvement would be my professional life. As a technical writer, I had ended up being involved in the process of document control, a function then usually found in the Quality organization. By the mid-80's I was involved in more general

Quality management. Under the wing of a friend, boss, and mentor, Mike Beveridge, I was privileged to learn hands-on how to initiate and maintain each of the basic quality systems necessary to manufacturing. Most of these systems were "in transition" in those days, moving from a world where the Quality Department was responsible for inspections and control to a world where the group who created quality (or lack of it) was also responsible for that quality.

I mentioned above that there are four primary inputs to my thinking, and I have covered the first two. The other two came to me in the early 1990's. The first of those two was a single phrase from Peter Senge's book The Fifth Discipline That phrase is "learning organization." It hit me with the same transformational force that "continuous improvement" had a decade earlier, and with good reason; continuous improvement demanded Senge's vision of a learning organization as the structure where culture, process, and knowledge, all optimized, could meet and mix in a synergistic spiral of success.

At approximately the same time I began a period of working with teams. Part of the success of the Japanese in their pursuit of quality had been through the use of work teams as drivers of continuous improvement. Before I go further, let me emphasize that I do not believe Japanese teams provide a good model for American teams. There is a profound cultural gap between the Japanese perception of the role of the individual in society and the American perception, and that gap is responsible, in my opinion, for many of the failures in work-team implementation in the United States. There is still, however, much to be learned from their success, especially in learning how to make groups of people more effective in making and implementing decisions.

Thus I come to the fourth of my primary inputs: the work of Dennis Romig, author of Breakthrough Teamwork and Side by Side Leadership. I have been fortunate to work extensively with Dennis and his colleagues in training teams and helping groups find structured ways to improve the efficiency and the effectiveness of their decision-making. A foundational element of Dennis' work is research he has done around a few fairly simple conclusions. Dennis has a simple but compelling set of requirements for the research data upon which he is willing to base his conclusions: the research must be done in real work environments (not academic simulations) and the research must have involved a control group. These two requirements make his conclusions credible well past the point of opinion. (Here you see my value for correctly analyzed data in action.)

These are some of the most important things I have learned and believe in. They have all led to the model I propose in this book: the Improvement Engine. Should you continue to read, I hope you will find in the following pages an explanation for how learning and trust are the primary shapers of the way we make things better—and making things better, it seems to me, really is what it's all about.

Chapter 1

What I'm Going to Tell You
"Get Ready. Hang onto Your Seat!"

"What does it matter how one comes by the truth so long as one pounces upon it and lives by it?"
Henry Miller

The title for this chapter comes from an old adage, well known among those who instruct others for a living, but for which I can find no particular, original source. The adage refers to a basic three-step process that should be kept in mind while designing instruction to ensure that participants gain the most from what is presented. It goes like this:

1) Tell them what you're going to tell them.
2) Tell them.
3) Tell them what you told them.

This does not mean that effective instructional design is simply a matter of hammering a point home through repetition. The first step should ensure that participants know what they are about to learn, what they will be able to do differently after they complete the instruction, and how they will be able to apply what they learn. The second step, of course, delivers the new knowledge required to perform new skills. The third step should validate that what was intended has been accomplished and, ideally, give participants an opportunity to put what they have learned in context for themselves. Step 2, obviously, we are all familiar with and

1

expect as part of the teaching process; steps 1 and 3, however, are often overlooked. That is unfortunate, for these are the steps that provide motivation and meaning, without which learning is seldom more than marginally successful. Accordingly, in keeping with this simple bit of instructor's wisdom, I will devote this first chapter to the relatively brief task of telling you what I'm going to tell you.

To get started on the Improvement Engine, I will introduce you to a set of equations I call the "Physics of Success." They will show how the foundation of success depends on learning and improvement. Once you are familiar with these equations, you will see that they form a rational basis for the concentration on learning and improvement that has been at the heart of the "quality revolution" in organizational (particularly business) practices since the latter half of the 20th century. While there is much to be learned from the equations themselves, their purpose in this book is fairly simple: to ensure that you are convinced of the need to pursue learning and improvement at least as vigorously as you pursue productivity and profit, since the latter are a product of the former.

Armed with this conviction, you will then be ready to learn about the Improvement Engine. The Improvement Engine is a phenomenon which manifests itself in every person, process, and organization. It is running right now inside your own mind, and it should be part of the reason you bought this book in the first place. It is running in your business. It is running in your family. It is running in every group with which you come together to pursue any common purpose.

As presented in this book, it is a fairly simple diagram that shows the foundational elements of the Physics of Success in action. The Engine is fueled by knowledge, curiosity, and hope, and it drives people to seek and act toward change. By searching and acting, they discover new knowledge, and the cycle repeats. As a model, it explains not only *what* works, but *why*—something often (mostly?) overlooked in the literature of continuous improvement.

Perhaps most importantly, it comprehends the human portion of the improvement process, explaining, if you will, the psychology of improvement—or at least the psychological factors which affect it. Organizationally, the Engine explains the connections that must exist to mesh Organizational Development and Human Relations issues with improvement tools and methods most commonly associated with Quality, Design, and Manufacturing issues. Without such a meshing, adoption of improvement processes such as Six Sigma or attempts to "change culture" tend to be unsuccessful. The Engine makes the reasons clear.

Analysis of the working of the Engine will lead to several specific actions that you can take to better manage improvement in any context, personal or organizational. Additionally, you will be able to use the Engine as a model to trace why your current efforts toward improvement are—or are not—meeting your own expectations.

I will reference data on human behavior that will reinforce the accuracy of this model. I will show how other improvement processes are comprehended, even explained in some ways, by the workings of the Engine. This information will help you to understand that you do not have to replace current, valid improvement processes with the Engine; you can simply overlay the Engine on what you currently do in order to understand how you may accelerate improvement using your current methods. The Engine will add value to your current methods by giving users more than a mere "recipe" for improvement. "Recipes"—step-by-step prescriptions for improvement—usually fail to provide the flexibility to comprehend every situation. Note that Six Sigma uses two different "recipes" for design (DMADV—Define, Measure, Analyze, Design, Verify) versus improvement of existing processes (DMAIC—Define, Measure, Analyze, Improve, Control). Models and equations, however, if they are correct, should apply more universally and allow more complete and accurate understanding of your situation.

Last but far from least, I will pay some particular attention to leadership in this context, since leadership itself may be seen to have the most impact on, and therefore the most responsibility for, the pursuit of improvement in organizations.

What, then, will you be able to do, or do better, as a result of reading this book? Here is the most concise list I can formulate:

1) Justify, for yourself and others, an increasingly passionate fixation on learning as the foundation of sustainable success. (Note that the same part of the inner brain that is responsible for learning new information, is also responsible for each person's ability to successfully adapt to change.)
2) Acknowledge and plan for the fact that few—if any—changes of a meaningful nature are accomplished without some change of human behavior. In order to accomplish improvement, project and process improvement leaders must change people as well as products, processes, and services.
3) Take specific, justifiable actions (several will be suggested) to increase the pace and quality of learning and improvement.
4) Use the Engine as an analytical tool to discover what systemic factors are supporting or hindering your efforts to improve.
5) Adjust—or build from scratch if necessary—a leadership philosophy, with corresponding actions, which comprehends the above and maximizes the results achieved thereby.

I think that's a fairly laudable set of objectives. Shall we begin?

Reflection:

(This is a section I will include at the end of each chapter. The purpose is to emphasize key points and to pose some questions for your consideration.)

- Improvement seems almost to have attained the status of religion in the last few decades. The phrase "continuous improvement"—which meant so much to me when first I heard it—may even be in danger of becoming cliché. For some, the word conjures a vision of people obsessively pursuing insignificant advances using oppressively inflexible methods. In such a mode, dissent is not viable; doubt is regarded suspiciously; compliance is politically correct.

- Can you, for the purpose of this book, hear the phrase "continuous improvement" again with "new ears"— hear it as though for the first time? There is still, I believe, some magic in that phrase. "Improvement," either as a word or as a concept, still refers to the idea that tomorrow can be better than today. That means hope, something I am sure you are unwilling to live without. Take a moment or two before you start reading in earnest to re-energize your emotional view of what "improvement" really means.

• Let's make sure you have some clear test issues of your own. You will want to be able to verify these concepts against your personal experience.

- Think of the three best and worst things you have done in trying to make a change, complete a project, etc.— an activity that involved (perhaps depended upon) the input/wok of others. Write those experiences down! As you read, use them consciously to test the ideas presented.

Chapter 2

Change, Learning, and Improvement

Lord C.: *"Can you see anything?"*
Carter: *"Yes. Wonderful things."*

(Exchange between Lord Carnarvon and Howard Carter on the occasion of the first glimpse into Tutankhamen's inner tomb)

I used to teach a one-hour introduction to quality to all incoming employees in the Austin, Texas site of a major electronics firm. The intent of the session was to give new employees some sense of how and why—and under what philosophies and assumptions—our quality systems had been developed and put in place. I also discussed how industry, and our company in particular, had experienced fundamental changes over the last two decades and how quality had been instrumental in causing those changes as well as bringing solutions to the problems created by those changes. Most of all, I just tried to get across a few critical concepts: that customer satisfaction is always the final measure of quality, that there are proven systems to help assure that products and processes achieve high customer satisfaction, and that we must always and forever seek improvement in everything we make and do.

As part of this session, I would write a word on the board: "Improvement." I would ask the class—and I ask you right now—do you believe in this? Of course, everybody always did, and I imagine you do as well. After all, life would seem a bit weary and bleak if there were not the possibility of making things better. Is not the very concept of hope dependent on the idea of improvement?

All right, so everybody thinks improvement is a good idea. Then, however, I would ask another question: "Can you have improvement without change?" Brows would furrow. Perhaps somebody would come up with the example of the untouched bottle of wine which improves simply by sitting around, to which I would reply, "The improvement in the wine is due to chemical changes during the aging." Brows would furrow some more, and soon heads would start shaking.

If you think about it, the answer is obvious through simple logic; improvement is by definition a change in condition, or at least perceptions of those conditions, so change <u>must</u> be a part of improvement. Are you as positive about change as you are about improvement? Doubtful—if you are like me, you have seen plenty of the negative effects of change as well, and come to justly fear them.

"So," I would say to the class, "change is absolutely a necessary part of improvement, but is the following true?" At this point, I would put an equal sign and the word "Change" to the right of the word "Improvement," thus:

Improvement = Change

Heads would begin to shake pretty quickly. No, change is not sufficient to be called improvement. "Well, if we treat this as an equation, is there <u>one thing</u> we could add to change that would always turn it to—or at least toward—improvement?" A short pause here—give them time to think about—and then I would ask: "Would this make the equation true?", and I would write the following:

Improvement = Change + Learning

For many years, I never had a person object to the validity of this equation. I propose it here as the first of four equations that I call the

Physics of Success. One more describing learning appears below and the other two are coming right up in the next chapter, but this one deserves a good bit of discussion, as I believe it is perhaps the most complicated of the four. Also, I believe that understanding it—truly grasping it, in the visceral, visual manner that I described in the foreword regarding my perceptions in high school of mechanics and optics equations—will be fundamental in helping you learn what I am trying to teach: a simple and predictable way to manage change in order to achieve success.

Think about the possible four scenarios suggested by the equation:

Improvement = Change + Learning

Scenarios/examples:

1) An unfavorable change occurs, and nobody learns how or why (change and learning are both negative). Obviously there is no improvement here.
2) A favorable change occurs, but nobody learns how or why (change positive, learning negative). This is a happy accident, but without learning, it is likely to be erased since nobody understands how to sustain the change. This can be called improvement only so far as the favorability of the change outweighs and/or outlasts the failure to learn from it.
3) An unfavorable change occurs, but the root cause is discovered (change negative, learning positive). Since the root cause is discovered, the unfavorable change may be reversed. Also, understanding of the root cause can lead to predictive planning, so that such unfavorable changes may be better anticipated and prevented in the future. In most cases, this is more productive and sustainable than the kind of possible improvement under scenario 2.
4) A favorable change occurs, and there is substantial knowledge about how and why (change and learning are both positive— this would especially apply in the case of successful, planned

changes). When positive change is accompanied by learning, there can be no doubt that improvement has been achieved.

Note in the above scenarios that positive learning has more of an impact in defining improvement than the change itself. (That is why scenario 3 has a more positive outcome than scenario 2.) This suggests that learning may be more important than the actual change activity itself. Think about the last project you were involved in planning. How much time was spent in planning activities necessary to complete the physical parameters of the project? How much time was spent on defining how individuals would learn about the change, how the change would be documented, or any other aspect of the organization's ability to learn the how and why of this change? In my experience, the bulk of the attention is on the planning of activity; it is usually about two-thirds of the way in before somebody says, "Hey, shouldn't we get Training involved in this? Maybe we need a class or something—and how about documentation?" All too often, the result of those questions is a request for a short ("Can't have them away from their jobs all day!") classroom session—usually the least effective way of achieving learning—and/or the generation of a lifeless specification.

If learning is potentially more critical to improvement than the activity of change itself, why would we spend the minority of our time planning it? There are two simple answers:

1) Learning is very hard to measure. There are volumes of literature that make this point abundantly clear. Since it is hard to measure, it is difficult to plan in the traditional timeline sense (start on this date, execute, end on that date). The activity of performing training may easily be set to a timeline, but doing the training and achieving the learning are two different matters. Remember too, as noted above, that training is usually expected to be delivered in classrooms, and this is seldom the most effective manner of teaching. Coaching, hands-on training, and mentoring are often more effective learning vehicles. Management follow-up

on training which ensures that employees use new skills in a real work environment immediately after they have been taught is probably the most important and most often overlooked factor in achieving a successful learning outcome.

2) Learning is at least partly a psychological process, so to deal with learning one must deal with emotions. (This will be dealt with much more fully when I discuss the Improvement Engine.) Most managers would rather be skinned. (To which, by the way, I say, "Tough." A manager's job is to manage performance. Emotions affect performance, despite desperate management proclamations that they shouldn't. Thus part of a manager's job is to manage emotions. Sorry.)

By the way, it might be useful to define "learning" here as well. For the purposes of this book, my definition of learning is as follows:

Learning—The assimilation of knowledge to support change in behavior.

That's right, I am saying that if knowledge is gained and <u>no change in behavior results, then there is no learning</u>. Some might argue that the study of theory and philosophy would therefore be invalidated as learning, since such study results in no change in behavior; I disagree. Study in the abstract, as well as the simple accumulation of factual information, can result in changes of behavior, for it can change the rational and factual bases upon which one makes decisions. Those decisions, based on the changed perceptions, will result in behavior different than it would have been before. Therefore, learning—according to the above definition—has occurred.

I have an equation form for this concept as well:

Learning = Communication + Application

Communication may, at its simplest, involve merely the telling and the hearing of new information. (It should be remembered that the hearing, not the telling, has most to do with how much communication actually occurred.) Application, however, requires at a minimum that the new knowledge gained from this information be allowed to have an effect on previous thinking. This would, as suggested above, at least affect decision-making and thus produce different behavior. Conscious and purposeful application of new knowledge will, of course, maximize the learning from new information. Consider the following statement regarding "operational definitions" from Deming's <u>Out of the Crisis</u>:

> "The only communicable meaning of any word, specification, instruction, etc. . . .
>
> is not what the writer . . . had in mind, but is instead, the result of application." (<u>Out of the Crisis</u>, Chapter 2, Point #10)

Communication must be measured by its result, not its intent. Learning, as it has communication as one of its components, must also be measured by its result, not its intent.

Additionally, application involves *doing*. In fact, in the context of the system of equations I am building, application *is* the doing—it is activity, and it is productivity. It is the form of energy that humans bring intentionally to this system. Change will inevitably happen in the system and power it in some direction, and much of the focus of my analysis of the system is on how that energy may be directed toward improvement (more on this coming shortly).

It must not be forgotten, however, that in order for anything useful to come of all this, *people must do things*: services must be rendered; widgets must be built. It is certainly true that much of the point of the improvement philosophies expounded over the last few decades has been to de-emphasize the focus on simple activity—to show that productivity by itself is an insufficient guarantee of continuing success. This de-emphasis has been necessary because of the deceptions created by the markets of the early twentieth century, where demand for new products alone helped ensure the success of anyone with the capability of providing them. The intensity of global competition and the advantages obtained by those pioneering the quality revolution required a "backlash" movement to turn the focus from activity alone to activity that continuously improves. There is, after all, a good deal of wisdom in the concept that modern success is of ten a result of working smarter, not harder. Productivity, though, must not be thought to be in any way insignificant or incidental; it is *not* a given. At its very root, it represents one of the most important of human characteristics: the intelligence and the willingness to *do something* to improve the quality of life.

. . . .

Let's stop for a minute here and think about the implications.

First of all, does this match your experience? Have you seen improvement efforts fail because no learning occurred? (An example might be "cultural" or "soft skill" training that was widely taught but never truly practiced because no real expectation was ever set by management that the skills would be used—or, especially, modeled by the organization's managers themselves.) Have you seen small changes make a big difference because they were widely or thoroughly learned? (An example might be changing meeting behaviors—doing things like adding agendas, minute-taking, and structured decision-making to the normal way of doing business.)

Does the improvement equation also make intuitive sense to you? Should learning and change be the components of improvement? (Perhaps the components should be multiplied instead of added, or perhaps more weight should be given to learning, as some of the above discussion suggests—if you feel better about that, I encourage you to mentally rewrite it for the rest of the book. I don't think it makes any difference when it comes to drawing conclusions about how to improve.)

Given your own experience in organizations, do you agree that if there is part of this equation that may have received insufficient attention, it is probably the learning component? Have you ever seen organizations that you thought were particularly good at improving? Do you, in retrospect, see a lot of learning (as learning was defined above) also taking place in those organizations? Think about projects you have been involved in that stood out, either as successes or failures. Do you see learning—or failed learning—as instrumental in making those projects remarkable?

In his book The Fifth Discipline, Peter Senge coined the phrase "learning organization." By this he meant an organization that continually re-invents itself to adapt to new market conditions, technology, etc. I propose that we seek further, to be a "wise" organization—one that uses its learning to change perspectives based on what has been learned. Have you seen learning fail to become wisdom? What is the cost of such failure?

Think about those things awhile. It might even be a good time to put the book down and reflect a bit. I'm about to start talking about change, and the next bit gets into some of that study of the abstract, as I was discussing above. I encourage you to take a while to let this sit, perhaps percolate a bit, and become valid for you.

. . . .

Now we need to talk about change. Change has gotten a lot of press in the last 20 years or so. The actual pace of change in the business world has increased and may still be increasing, mirroring the exponential increase in human knowledge and fueled by competition that has become global in even the most mundane markets. Thousands of conference rooms have echoed with phrases like "change management" and "embracing change." Certainly the ability to "manage change" is touted as providing a rather broader competitive advantage in today's world, especially as compared to an older world where we perceive that there was more stability (or was it inertia?). Just a few paragraphs ago, I told you that I am hoping to teach you "a simple and predictable way to manage change in order to achieve success." I will try to avoid some trouble right now by telling you that by "manage" I do not mean "control." "Control" connotes an absolute level of predictability which can seldom be achieved when dealing with change, and is, in fact, seldom desired in achieving improvement through change and learning. "Manage" is a word with some flexibility around it. Change management requires learning. Then change plus learning can yield improvement.

I think that the most successful enterprises have been managing change effectively for a long time. That, in fact, is what has probably made them successful, as Chapter 3 will make clear. In the last 20 to 30 years, though, competition and the practice of continuous improvement techniques have increased not only the pace of change but also the focus on change itself.

I have come to regard change as a form of energy. The title of this book refers to the "Physics of Success"; I propose that change is the energy which fuels this particular branch of "physics." The different disciplines of physics such as kinetics, optics, and thermodynamics are each built around the understanding of some form of energy—in the case of the aforementioned disciplines, motion, light, and heat, respectively. In each of the disciplines, we have learned to express that understanding precisely through mathematics, with the result that we can not only explain but also accurately <u>predict</u> their behavior in a wide range of situations. (In keeping with the tradition of applying Greek to the naming of the disciplines of physics, we could call the physics of change "morphics." I will not force the term on you as a condition of further reading, but I reserve the right to use it once or twice more as a simple catch phrase. Honestly, I think I am rather intimidated by the idea of presuming to name such a thing.)

Now, wouldn't it be nice if we could predict the behavior of change? What prevents us from doing so, if it is indeed a form of energy like those above?

Three things prevent us from predicting the behavior of change, and they are closely related. First of all, predicting the behavior of change requires predicting human behavior, since the changes we are interested in mostly involve humans. Remember, as I mentioned above, that humans are always introducing the energy of application to their environment; they are always doing things. Humans introduce too much randomness to the systems with which they interact to allow for observing and isolating the behavior of change itself. The last half of that sentence also points to the second reason we can't predict change: we don't have a way to measure it. The third reason is a consequence to some degree of the second; we have no family of equations to describe the behavior of change.

All of the energies we have harnessed we have also learned how to measure. We measure speeds, wavelengths, temperatures, voltages, and pressures. Note that we have no way to directly measure gravity. We understand something about it by watching its effects on the motion of bodies, but we can't actually measure it, and we certainly can't harness it. Our relationship with change as an energy form is much the same as with gravity; we know it's there, we can see it working, we can even measure its effect, but we can't actually measure change itself.

Change is rather a constant condition. It is the result—in a Newtonian transfer-of-energy sense—that comes from the release of all the other forms of energy. All of the energies that make up our current understanding of physics cause change. In addition, change results from expenditures of <u>emotional and intellectual energy</u>.

It is a curious paradox that, as the objects and energies of the universe seek equilibrium—a condition where no change occurs—they cause change. The very search for constancy begets change. It is doubly ironic that we are a species whose success has been largely due to our ability to control, to some degree, the effects of fortune upon us through applying our intelligence and instituting purposeful, planned change (e.g., building houses and dams, creating laws and governments, writing books, etc.). We minimize the damage change causes us by changing our environment to better protect us. It should not be surprising that fear of loss of control is one of the most insidious and unrecognized emotions in the human gamut. Our almost instinctive resistance to change is linked to this fear and will, as you shall see when we discuss the Improvement Engine, be a key factor in how organizations succeed or fail in their efforts to improve.

Change is also chaotic in its nature. Like the explosion of ignited gasoline, change will release a great deal of various energies, and unless that release is to some degree harnessed and directed, the result is most likely to be destructive to our own ends. Let us look more to the positive side of this comparison, however. Ignited gasoline has, in fact, been well harnessed and directed through various devices, notably the internal combustion engine. Learning may be interpreted as the only "control" we can apply to change, and despite the difficulties involved in its measurement, it may be the best indicator of an organization's capability and capacity for managing change. Remember, humans are successful because they have explored the unknowns and taken the risks that allowed them to create such marvels as the internal combustion engine. Perhaps a better understanding of the "physics" that involve change, and an Engine to harness them, will enable us to fear change a little less.

Reflection:

(Many of the topics in this chapter will have to be re-examined a bit after you have been introduced to the remaining equations of "morphics" and the Improvement Engine itself. I apologize in advance for any seeming redundancy; the intent is to help you look at the same questions through different and growing perspectives.)

- Improvement requires change combined with learning. Learning is the more overlooked and possibly the more important of these two elements.

- Consider the learning systems in your organization. Do they rely primarily on classroom training? Are there opportunities to improve the quality of learning simply by using alternative methods such as coaching or mentoring?

- Are supervisors, managers, and executives measured on their ability to develop the capabilities of their staff? Are they expected to <u>rigorously</u> ensure that new learning has a chance to be immediately practiced? Do their immediate superiors highlight occasions when new learning by their staff will require change of behavior (e.g., modeling the behavior or leading execution of new techniques) by that staff's supervision?

- Is learning carefully considered and designed as a part of each project? Is the same rigor applied to that planning as to the listing and scheduling of required activities?

- Change is a powerful, chaotic force just as likely to destroy as to build. It is natural to fear and/or resist change to some degree.

  - What is your own attitude toward change? Recognizing that improvement absolutely requires change, do you comfortably accept that change will never end if you seek a state or outcome better than today's?

  - It is often easy to recognize when change would benefit systems, products, and other people's performance or attitudes. How good are you at recognizing—and accepting and pursuing—change that is required of you in beliefs, habits, and actions?

17

Chapter 3

The Physics of Success

"Progress, far from consisting in change, depends on retentiveness. When change is absolute there remains no being to improve and no direction is set for possible improvement: and when experience is not retained, as among savages, infancy is perpetual. Those who cannot remember the past are condemned to repeat it."

George Santayana

We have established two equations that I propose as the foundation of the Physics of Success. They are:

- **Improvement = Change + Learning**
- **Learning = Communication + Application**

Note that the lower equation defines one component that is then used in the equation above it, so that the ability to define the simplest concept (learning) builds toward the ability to define a more complicated and meaningful concept: improvement. The lower equation is perhaps more of a definition than a proper equation of a discipline of physics; note that change, the source of energy in this discipline, is not mentioned in the definition of learning. So perhaps the equation describing improvement is actually the first in the hierarchy of equations that I call the Physics of Success. The remaining two equations, to be introduced shortly, will continue to build this hierarchy.

"Build toward what?" would be a reasonable question to ask. In truth, improvement itself is a worthy end goal, is it not?

Yes, but we must avoid the temptation to stop and worship solely at the altar of improvement. Despite all the focus on this topic for the last few decades, we must remember that improvement alone is not the purpose of organizations. In the last chapter, I mentioned that harnessing and directing the energies of ignited gasoline were necessary to derive safe and predictable results. The same is true of change, and I would say that describing improvement only harnesses change; it provides no direction. We could spend a lifetime in improving that which is irrelevant to our real purpose.

We need more than mere improvement; we need <u>progress</u>. As you consider the two words, do you sense the difference—and the importance of that difference? Have you seen people or organizations obsessed with getting better at something that doesn't really make that much difference to their customers? It is often a manifestation of our resistance to change that we focus on improving the minutiae of what we already do rather than changing—or even abandoning—what we have done for years.

Imagine the class I described at the beginning of Chapter 2. This time, though, the word on the board is "progress," not "improvement." And the question asked is, "Can you have progress without improvement?" The answer, again, is quite obviously "no." So improvement is certainly a component of progress, but the following equation would be incomplete:

Progress = Improvement

So what must be added to improvement to turn it into progress? The answer, as implied above, has something to do with direction, does it not? I propose the following:

Progress = Improvement + Shared Vision

When you direct change, as harnessed by learning, to become improvement that leads toward a purpose, you achieve progress.

Without shared vision, members of an organization may make any number of unproductive mistakes. They may, as mentioned above, pursue the perfection of irrelevant details. Even worse, they may engage in activity that distracts from or is antithetical to the very purpose of the organization.

The importance of vision has been hammered home by enough authors and consultants that I will not dwell long on it. It is probably appropriate, however, to point out the continuing relevance of an example of the power of vision that is frequently mentioned by those same authors and consultants: John F. Kennedy's "moon goal." In 1961, President Kennedy set the United States on the path to the moon with a single speech that galvanized an entire nation to put a man on the moon (and, notably, return him safely to Earth) by the end of the decade. For those few years, it seemed, citizens of the U.S. could unite in the pursuit of that goal, though other forces such as racial and generational issues made for fractious times.

A compelling vision is a powerful tool, and when it is skillfully wielded in pursuit or defense of shared values, it can move millions to action. Many organizational reforms begin with establishing a set of three critical concepts: vision, mission, and values. Vision is the imagined state of the organization at some future point: its size, its wealth, its influence, the nature and needs of its customers, etc. Mission is the activity on which the organization will focus in order to achieve that vision. Values are the guidelines and boundaries that the organization places on behavior that will be considered acceptable and/or laudable in pursuit of the mission and the vision.

In the above equation, I ask you to include mission and values as parts of vision. In imagining an ideal state for an organization, it makes sense to me that we must include what the organization does and that it does so within accepted standards of behavior.

So now these three equations tell us that in order to achieve progress, we must focus on rigorously planned learning, couple that with change activities to achieve improvement, and direct that improvement toward an ideal state within behavioral boundaries defined by law, ethics, and our own conscience. This is actually getting pretty complicated, but the equations, by condensing all these components, make it easier to grasp and visualize. (At least they do for me, and I hope they do for you as well. That is rather the point of having created them.)

While the build-up of components is getting more complicated, however, note that what we are adding—vision in this case, with visionary goals—is actually easier to measure than many of the components at the lower end of the equation hierarchy. After all, it is pretty easy for you to determine whether or not your organization has a vision, and whether it has a mission, and whether or not there is a shared set of values. You may wonder about their quality, but their existence is pretty much a "digital" decision; either they exist or they do not. (Hint: are they in writing?) Measuring their quality is more or less a matter of measuring your own personal satisfaction with them. If they satisfy your need to understand what you should do, and how it is permissible to behave, in order to move your organization forward, then the quality is at least adequate.

But progress, like improvement, is not an adequate final goal. The history of failed organizations is filled with stories of progress which, through misfortune or mismanagement, proved insufficient to keep the organization alive. The end goal of all this must be what we call "success."

Imagine the board again at the front of the class. This time the word on the board is "success." And the first question posed is, "Is progress a necessary component of success?" I would hope that I do not have to argue long for an affirmative answer to this question. A very temporary success might be achieved by a static organization, or by the one-time release of a "home run" product, but if you have even picked up this book, I would think that is not the type of success in which you are interested. Success, it seems to me, must be a sustainable state. So again, the board now shows an incomplete equation:

Success = Progress

And the next question is, "What must we add to progress in order to achieve success?"

The first part of the answer is actually a bit brutally simple: we must add that which allows us to keep making progress: profit.

Success = Progress + Profit

This is not intended to be simply a mathematical justification of capitalism. Profit may, after all, be defined fairly broadly as a component of success in this context. As I said above, it need only be that which allows an organization to continue to make progress. In the business world, this amounts primarily to well-understood resources like capital, equipment, and personnel, all of which translate mostly to money. A religious organization might regard profit in very different terms, however—an increase in converted souls, for instance. In such a case, inspiration might be a more valued resource and salvation a more important definition of "profit" than money. In either case, however, it is undeniably and critically true that without profit, the organization will eventually die.

I would also point out that, as in the previous equation, that which we have added to the hierarchy of components is even easier to measure. Especially in business, measuring profit is fairly straightforward. "Creative accounting" may confuse the case a bit, but shareholders and the market cannot be deceived by such tactics in any sustainable manner. At the end of the day, the question, "Did you make money?" is pretty easy to answer.

Finally, profit is not really something toward which you may take any particular action, except by pursuing learning, improvement, productivity, and thus progress. Even the simple act of cost-cutting, which one might regard as direct action on profit, is in fact change performed with the hope of improving profit margins. Remember that I am assuming you seek *sustainable* success. In that light, it is critical to remember that profit is a result of success in what you have already done; only progress will provide for success in what you have yet to do.

This equation requires one more factor to be complete. That factor has probably occurred to some of you already. Our level of success will also depend on how much we are able to do, thus:

Success = Progress + Profit + Productivity

Yes, at the end of the day, you actually have to do something to be successful, and hopefully, the more you do it, the more successful you will be. Note that this component is also highly measurable. Most organizations have spent a good deal of time understanding this component of their success, although even here, it may be questionable how sufficient those metrics are for determining success. These measures typically measure activity; they are sometimes inadequate for defining accomplishment.

Let us look at the entire set of equations now:

- **Success = Progress + Profit + Productivity**
- **Progress = Improvement + Vision**
- **Improvement = Change + Learning**
- **Learning = Communication + Application**

Another look at this may be had by adding all the minor components together to achieve the end result:

Success = Communication + Application + Change + Vision + Profit + Productivity

As in the disciplines of physics, a very complex concept, success, is defined by a host of smaller components. Also, as in physics, you must achieve understanding of the lesser components before you can get to the greater. Thus not only the list, but also the order of the above components is important. You must first have communication. If you add application, you have learning and may proceed to improvement by adding change. From there you may achieve progress if you can add vision. Finally, success is a matter of making a profit by doing all of these things together—and in this order. In my own mind, this very much resembles a hierarchy of equations relative to mechanics in traditional physics:

- $W = Fd$ [work = (force) x (distance)]
- $F = ma$ [force = (mass) x (acceleration)]
- $a = \Delta v/t$ [acceleration = (change in velocity) / (time)]
- $v = d/t$ [velocity = (distance) / (time)]

Each equation, starting from the bottom, establishes a definition that is then used by the equation above it to define a more complex concept. The result is finally a mathematical understanding of "work"—a very complex concept indeed.

There are a few important differences between the two sets of equations, however. First of all, each of the equations in the Physics of Success adds new components not previously used, whereas the mechanics equations use time twice (in defining velocity and acceleration) and distance twice (in defining velocity and work). Also, as I have mentioned earlier, I am not certain that the mathematical relations and proportions are exactly correct. These equations are in their infancy; perhaps with more research and empirical observation they may be refined, but I believe that I have correctly identified the components and the order of their relation. As such, they are well enough established that we may at least begin learning from them.

A more important difference is this: in the case of the equations dealing with motion, there is no significant difference in the measurability or the comprehensibility of the bottom components as compared with the upper ones. Time and distance are relatively easy to measure and understand, as are mass and change in velocity. As I have already noted, the same cannot be said for the components which lead to success. Those at the bottom of the hierarchy, especially change and communication, are practically immeasurable and thus make learning and improvement difficult to understand—and thus more difficult to achieve, since one must pursue them without any absolute certainty about when or whether they have been attained. (Perhaps this is true only from a modern perspective. We have enjoyed the benefits of rulers, scales, and timepieces of one sort or another for thousands of years. Before necessity forced their invention, it may well be that ancient thinkers struggled with those concepts as I do with these. Modern devices such as speedometers and pressure gauges allow for very easy measurement of speed and force. Perhaps with a few more thousands of years behind us, we may develop "changeometers" and "improvement gauges." It seems doubtful, but one may hope . . .) Application, especially in the guise of productivity, is probably the easiest of the lower components to measure, although the systems to measure it may be quite complex. Vision is somewhat easier to measure, and compared to the rest, profit is a cinch. Thus progress and success are easier to grasp—but *only if* you have already achieved learning and improvement.

The implication here is profound. If you want to achieve success, the bulk of your attention and resources should be focused on that which is most difficult to achieve—and to measure—on the path to success: learning and improvement. Also, as I mentioned above in my discussion on profit and progress, there is really almost no direct action you can take on profit except to enact change, which puts you again in the lower portion of the hierarchy: improvement and learning. The same is true for progress; the only direct action you can take to affect progress that would rise above learning and improvement would be to establish or revise your vision—and even this would probably have to be regarded as improvement.

Now I will make what I believe to be an extraordinary claim: <u>I have just demonstrated that there is a mathematical relation between success and improvement, and that this relationship demands learning as one of its most critical components</u>. The equations—even in their infant state—and the logic prove it conclusively. This is why the terms "continuous improvement" and "learning organization" first excited me and should, even after years of use, overuse, and abuse, still excite you; learning and improvement establish the *necessary* path to sustainable success. Those who have championed these concepts have understood intuitively the truth of that; the Physics of Success makes that understanding more a matter of engineering-styled proof. I hope my father would be proud.

Reflection:

- In the pursuit of success, it is tempting to focus on that which is most easily understandable (e.g., controlling costs, building revenue, executing activities according to a timeline, etc.). The equations of the Physics of Success make plain, however, that none of these things actually happen without a foundation of learning, change, and improvement.

  - Are your organization's energies properly focused, in light of this conclusion? How well can your organization adapt to the fact that some of its most important energies must be expended on that which is difficult or impossible to measure?
  - Think of a major project in your organization that succeeded. How do you see these equations played out in the way the project was initiated, managed, executed, and finalized?
  - Repeat the last question for a project that failed.

- Vision is the harness that directs improvement into the path of progress.

  - Does your organization have a clearly articulated vision? Does that vision include mission and values?
  - If there is a vision, is it really, honestly inspiring? Have you ever actually referred to it to make a decision about how or whether to do something?

- Beyond the hype, "continuous improvement" and "learning organization" are still important terms representing vital components of sustainable success.

  - Take some time to re-acquaint yourself with them. Try to see them as though for the first time. Let them sink in. Let them inspire you.
  - Aren't you happy to find somebody still referring to profit while talking about all this improvement and learning?

Chapter 4

Building the Improvement Engine

"It is possible to fly without motors, but not without knowledge and skill."
Wilbur Wright

"In order that all men may be taught to speak truth, it is necessary that all likewise should learn to hear it."
Samuel Johnson

In the glory days of the classic automobile, companies like Duesenberg and Bugatti didn't really sell you a complete car. They sold you instead just a chassis and an engine. A separate company fabricated the body according to specifications provided by the automobile manufacturer, with instructions from the customer about how that body and the interior were to be customized to the customer's expectations. This book bears a certain resemblance to that arrangement. It "sells" you an "engine"—the Improvement Engine—and a "chassis" of supporting logic and principles. From there it will be up to you to design and build the "body", and by this I mean to form and fit the processes, goals, and values of your organization around the "engine" and "chassis" in such a way as to pursue your vision. Looking back on the equations of the Physics of Success, you might say that the Improvement Engine will give you a system that is an engineered solution based on the first equations defining learning and improvement. It will allow you to better understand how to engage these in the pursuit of progress. You, of course, are the only one who can supply vision, the other necessary element of progress. But with your vision, and with the Improvement Engine as a power plant fueled by change, the road to success will be a little easier to travel.

I originally called the Improvement Engine a "learning model," because at first, that was what I was trying to define. I was looking for a way to graphically illustrate the way organizations learn. In this chapter, I plan to take you step-by-step through the process of creating the original "learning model" as well as its evolution to the Improvement Engine. This chapter will focus on *why* the Engine runs—how "morphics" (there's that word again) are empirically illustrated by the working of the Improvement Engine. Not until later chapters will I begin to really discuss *how* the Engine runs—how performance may be adjusted and affected. Obviously, both are equally important. However, if you are the impatient type, or if you tend to prefer pragmatic application to ethereal theory, you might be tempted to skip this chapter. After all, you don't need to really understand a good deal about the workings of a V8 in order to drive a car powered by one. It's mostly a matter of knowing how to work the accelerator and when to add fuel and oil. Remember, however, that you are going to be responsible for some portion of your vehicle's final design and construction, as I mentioned above. Trying to do so without some understanding of theory might lead to mistakes that would adversely affect your drive to success.

I began building my "learning model" by trying to list the steps— perhaps they are phases—involved in the part of organizational behavior that can most obviously be called "learning"—that is, the process of invention. I finally settled on the following three:

1) Innovation—Innovation is the idea of the invention itself, the very spark of imagination within somebody's brain that ignites the whole creative process. It might be an idea for a new product or service, or a potential way to improve a process, or a new

marketing concept. It can be anything—*anything*—that causes somebody to want to create change.

2) Design—Design, in this context, is something that starts taking place as soon as any attempt is made to add substance to the basic idea. Design starts happening before any word is spoken or any drawing put on paper. It is, potentially, a completely internal process to the innovator. As one imagines the list of features for a new product, or fleshes out the complete set of steps in a new process, or considers what slogans might best communicate a new marketing strategy, one begins to design. As soon as a sketch is made on a napkin, design work has started.

3) Deployment Data—This might seem an odd term to appear here. "Innovation" and "design" have a creative ring about them, but "deployment data" sounds a bit prosaic, doesn't it? It might be useful to remind you that I was thinking about organizational behavior here; in an organization, even the smallest one, ideas have to be communicated in order to be applied. In practice, in large organizations especially, there is often a very formal process and set of requirements (e.g., a specification for a design package) defining how ideas must be communicated to other groups responsible for their implementation. In any case, an invention which is not communicated is merely a wish or a dream. Some measure of control must be established over ideas in order to make them realities.

As I listed this last step, I realized that I did not want to stop with describing just the invention part of organizational learning, because that certainly wasn't where learning stopped. By listing these three steps, I had begun the process of invention I had just described, and doing so had made it quite clear that this was only a beginning. The fledgling bit of innovation in my mind, however, had only conceived a sort of circular repetition of these steps. Now that they were in front of me, I saw that this first vision was quite incomplete. The creation of deployment data did not allow a simple return to innovation. There must be feedback to spur improvement of the original idea, and that feedback had to come from what happens when inventions are released to be manufactured and distributed, to be used or to languish, to succeed or to fail.

What, I then asked myself, are the steps (or phases) that happen subsequent to release of deployment data? Again I found three:

1) Implementation—The requirements of the deployment data are put into practice. Tools and processes are modified to generate components that meet the physical requirements of the specification. Workers are trained to new procedures. Production goals and schedules are generated. Sales forces make appointments and meet with prospective customers. Everything that was theoretical is translated into pragmatic action.

2) Experience—All of the above activity generates knowledge—a special kind of knowledge based on empirical results. Everything in the world of invention was based on what *should* happen; now it is time to see what *does* happen.

3) Application Data—From experience comes a flood of data. The data may seem to validate or refute theory; it may even seem to do both. The volume of data may be so vast as to obstruct the search for meaning. The data may be confounded and corrupted by inaccurate measurement, inadequate sampling plans, simple misinterpretation, and even falsification or its evil second cousin, "spin." Sometimes, blessedly though rarely in my experience, the data may present overwhelmingly obvious implications. The existence of the data is, however, undeniable—and its potential value is immense, provided that correct meaning (truth) can be extracted <u>and communicated</u>.

As I completed this list of steps, I realized I had something that looked and felt pretty much like the traditional interaction of product groups with manufacturing groups that had been a part of most of my working life. Product groups came up with ideas, worked them out as designs, and then set up a formal design package that they delivered to a manufacturing organization. The manufacturing organization, in turn, translated the design package into a process with individual machine recipes for each step, produced parts, kept records, and generated reports and summaries of data. Some portion of that data, where it was deemed relevant, was fed back to the product group to fuel improvements in future revisions of the product. I also saw, however, that this cycle was implied for most organizational interactions. Customers "invent" needs, often expecting application guidance from the supplier. The supplier then jumps immediately into "inventing" as well by creating a solution for the customer ("You need an air conditioner of such-and-such size," or "Our Triklon 3700 will do that for you if you simply upgrade your operating system."), hoping that the potential customer will become that most important of appliers, the paying customer.

You might remember that I was trying to get to a graphic representation of how learning happened. This is probably where I came to my first version of that graphic, and it looked something like this:

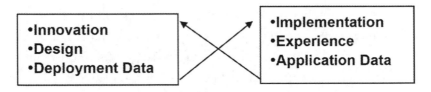

I immediately realized that while the system diagrammed above accurately described what happened with purely internal knowledge, it ignored the input of knowledge from new and theoretical sources. At first I showed that knowledge strictly as an input to the left-hand side of the diagram:

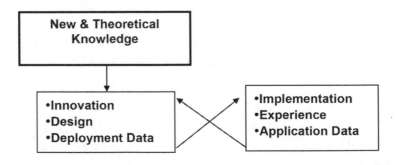

Then I realized that those same sources of knowledge are also informing the activity on the right-hand side of the diagram as well. This might simply be considered another type of invention and so be already comprehended by the diagram in its current state, but I also realized that this was, in a sense, an organizational diagram as well as a systems diagram, and I wanted to honor the ability of implementing groups (in my experience, the manufacturing organization) to apply new and theoretical knowledge to the immediate solution of problems faced in implementing theoretical specifications. Thus came version 3 of the diagram:

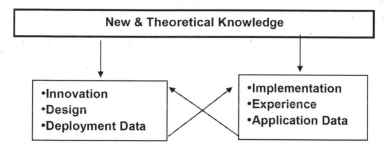

This diagram adequately and accurately described what I had observed for years: an "over the wall" approach to interaction between innovation and implementation. For anyone not familiar with the term, "over the wall" refers to a system where, for example, designers create packages telling how to build what they have created, and then, effectively, "throw" those packages over a "wall" to an organization which must then interpret and implement those instructions with almost no interaction from the designers. Although the focus of the term is usually on the delivery of designs, in organizations where this sort of separation is maintained and rewarded, this metaphorical wall often works just as effectively the other way; information about the manufacturability of the design is thrown back over the wall with little explanation or interaction—and often with a bit of finger-pointing attached, which usually adds an inch or two to the wall. Despite the wall, however, I felt this also accurately described how organizations learned. The height of the wall would be a gating factor in the organization's ability to learn. This diagram is what I first called my "learning model."

For those who may at this point be wondering how all this generates Productivity (an already proven necessary component of Success), you will need to consider the above diagram in three dimensions. Imagine an "axle" coming out of the application side of the diagram and receding into the page. When we "apply," we do things; we are productive. Thus all of that "applying" is actually generating value, products and services. The better and faster we mange the cycle of innovation and application, the more productive we are, the more value we add. This is the real output of the system.

There was one more factor I wanted to bring to this diagram, something I had observed when I first worked with an organization in establishing the use of statistical process control (SPC) in a manufacturing environment. The whole point of SPC is to use historical data from a process in order to understand the natural pattern of the results of that process. Once the natural pattern is understood, it becomes relatively easy to locate *un*natural results. By reacting to these—determining their root cause and implementing improvements to eliminate their future occurrence—the capability of a process to produce acceptable results may be improved. Most amazing to me, the use of this single, simple tool had a host of marvelous impacts on the culture of the organization itself. Since the organization had a better understanding of the actual capability of a process, there was less of a tendency to blame somebody—usually a hapless tool operator—when processes produced unacceptable results (e.g., out-of-specification parts) that were obviously a natural part of the historical pattern of results from that process. When such occasions arose, engineers, operators, supervisors, maintenance technicians, and managers were all inclined to look for something more productive than blame: a way to improve the process to forever avoid its latest failure. (Note that, since SPC also highlighted unusually *good* performance, it helped us identify best practices as well.) Not only was the object of their focus more productive; so were their methods. Because they all believed that SPC would point them to real problems or opportunities, they laid aside the usual tools of inter-departmental finger-pointing and instead used a collaborative approach to finding causes and determining the solution. SPC was itself an equal-opportunity, unbiased finger-pointer, and that finger was found to be reliable. The finger pointed at the process, though, not at the people. Data and decision making tools used in meetings helped build consensus (defined in the organization as a solution which all would agree to and support) as opposed to agenda-based and competitive "camps." With blame out of the picture, listening to everybody's ideas about how to fix the problem seemed to come naturally. Engineers who had previously ignored or at best given scant interest to input from maintenance technicians, since their input was usually anecdotal or based on "hunches," started to solicit their ideas. Production personnel who distrusted the "help" of engineers, since those engineers showed little understanding or sympathy toward their complaints about processes with problems—and had in the past been advocates of "cockpit error" as the cause of too many problems—found those same engineers more curious and interested when SPC data confirmed their grievances. Management reinforced all this change by focusing on the SPC results, not on blame or denial. Their position was constant: "SPC says we have a problem. That means the process has a problem. All of you own part of the process. Now all of you FIX IT!" It also helped that SPC often pointed to problems *before* processes started producing unacceptable material. Since identifying problems thus no longer required expensive losses, management exhibited a good deal less anxiety—and passed less of it on to those who had to fix the problems. Even the processes themselves gained a sort of credibility; if their performance was not up to expectations, at least they now seemed more predictable and less like black boxes into which one inserted millions of dollars of material with only hope, instead of some level of assurance, that it would return a successful result.

Do you see that cultural change in the light of the Physics of Success? Can you point to it in the hierarchy of equations? The change is reflected in the two lower equations. First of all, a critical change took place in the nature of communication. SPC results became a new and reliable part of the communication process. Second, the collaborative approach to root-cause fixes for problems led to increased learning, both because more people experienced the learning and because the solutions tended to address the actual causes of the problems instead of merely bandaging the symptoms. Better communication plus increased learning means more improvement, which leads to more and faster progress, which creates a higher level of success.

The spur to all this had been simply a new way to communicate. In terms of the system diagram above, it meant that a new way had been found to use deployment data and application data, especially the latter. The two had found a meeting place where innovation could be spurred by reliable information, and bearers of bad news from the application side could be confident that the information would be valued as a learning tool instead of as justification to shoot the messenger. Also, new ideas to fix the problems could be shared and were generally welcomed by all. It all had to do with data and a safe place to study it. Once I put this in the diagram, I felt for the first time that I was beginning to represent the model for real learning and improvement in an organization. I labeled the space in the diagram "Data Driven Improvement Methods." That, I felt, was the best way to describe functionally what had happened to focus the organization on learning—and thus improving—from its problems. Data from either function of the organization, innovation or implementation, could be safely brought to this space, and the learning generated there could be fed back (or forward, as the case may be) to both functions to generate improved future designs and implement better current solutions. All the while, new and theoretical knowledge streamed in to feed the learning frenzy. The wall over which so many unproductive things had been thrown was breached by the simple introduction of reliable, predictive data.

So now the diagram looked like this:

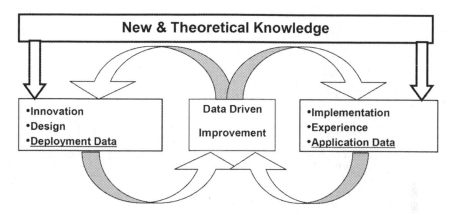

Although I did not yet know enough to rename it, I had now gone beyond the "learning model" I had first envisioned. In retrospect, I can now see that the addition of that central block had transformed this to the first version of the Improvement Engine.

What happens in the center box of the Improvement Engine? On the innovation side, expectations should be filtered by data on capabilities so that our ideas do not exceed our resources. The use of objective, trustworthy information should help build the momentum required for implementation. Creativity must be energized, and careful planning undertaken to harness it. On the application side, results must be carefully and objectively analyzed. Interpretation of data should lead to collaborative improvement—not blame and politics.

I will have one more very important addition to this diagram before I am finished building it, but it took me a while to find it, and before I did I had some key revelations from its current state. The introduction of that last part will not come until Chapter 6, because we have much to discuss about the model-about-to-be-Engine in its current state. Accordingly, I will pause here to discuss the implications of the diagram as it now stands.

First of all, remember that this Engine is <u>always</u> running. Human sentience being what it is, we simply can't stop learning. We observe our world, see things we like and things we don't, see things that work and things that don't; we draw conclusions and act on them. With every piece of information, with every contemplated action, the human mind is attempting to learn, even if it must battle its own tendency toward apathy, or the sheer unwillingness of the personality to learn the lessons at hand. The Engine is running in your organization right now, and your organization is learning new things every second. If that sounds good, wait for the *caveat*: they may not be learning what you would hope. You undoubtedly hope they are examining the outside world and their own working world with an eye to building their productivity and the organization's success. They are undoubtedly learning some other things, however. Some may be learning how to make poor performance look better than it really is or how to protect themselves from internal attacks. Some are undoubtedly learning the techniques required for mastery of the seventh level of *Doom*. Everyone is learning about each other: whom to talk to, whom to listen to, whom to imitate. Some may even be learning how to build a business just like this, but a bit better . . . One of an organization's greatest challenges—recognized by the current popularity of the term "alignment" in reference to an organization's goals and actions—is to maximize the learning of its member that is relevant to the organization's values, vision, mission, and goals. I will focus on this concept of "relevant learning" a good deal more after the Engine is completed. For now, remember that there is no challenge involved in starting the Engine; the challenge comes in managing its fuel (information) and controlling its direction. More on this later, however; let's get a look at what we have so far.

Consider the environments in which innovation and implementation take place and some of the natural cultural differences between organizations that exist in those environments. If your experience matches mine, you will have observed that groups focusing on innovation are fundamentally different in their approach to decisions than groups focusing on implementation. The innovators tend, quite naturally, to focus on creativity and originality as the characteristics which define more attractive alternatives. They tend to be early adopters of new technology and ideas. They are apt to approach problems from a theoretical perspective, trying to predict what *should* happen in a given set of circumstances. They may be impatient with details, preferring to take the 50,000 foot view as opposed to that from 1,000 feet to ground level. They like to leave flexibility in their plans so that they can react to unexpected circumstances and ideas. To outsiders (especially the group directly responsible for implementing their creations), they may appear to be "dreamers" or be regarded as unwilling to focus on the practical and unable to perceive the necessary.

The implementers, on the other hand, like to use data and predictability to guide their decisions. They like equipment and processes with proven performance and reliability. When trying to solve problems, they tend toward an empirical approach; they want data, history, and more data. They want detailed plans defining who will do what by when in order to accomplish specific goals. To outsiders (especially those directly responsible for providing them with designs and ideas to put into practice), they may appear to be demanding and obsessively attached to commitment.

These differences are a product of two inevitable facts. First, these are natural temperamental differences that can be detected as patterns by any number of personality profiling instruments (translation: people are just built that way). Second, and somewhat more interesting, they are the natural result of the state of resources in their respective work environments. On the innovation side of the above diagram, especially in the actual innovation phase before even the limits of design have been applied, *resources are essentially limitless*. They should be confined only by the imagination. Your reaction here may be, "Yes, but they have to limit themselves to some reasonable level of practicality, don't they?" True, but that level is only that which is theoretically possible—and that sort of leaves the door wide open, doesn't it? And honestly, if an idea were good enough, and if theory suggested strongly enough that it would work, wouldn't a board of directors be willing to approve anything they could to make that dream a reality?

Now consider the resources on the implementation side of the diagram. From the very moment implementation commences, *everything* is about limited resources. You may remember the focus on who, what, and when mentioned above. That focus is all about limited resources. From the minute they get a design package, they are faced with constraints in personnel, limited equipment, limited availability of that equipment, and that greatest and most implacable of all constraints: a finite amount of time. Add to that the constant pressure to control costs, and you have a work environment dominated by the concept of limitations.

Take a moment to really think how pervasive the effect of these two different environments is. Compare it, if you will, to the difference (at least the stereotypical difference) between the children of the depression and the children of the baby boom. Think what gaps of understanding and communication can build between such groups, and how those gaps, if left unconsidered and untended, can lead to resentment and open lack of respect. It is likely you have seen such conditions develop between groups. Look back at the Improvement Engine and think what damage can be done to it by the consequences of such differences. The importance of that structured, safe place for pursuing the common goal of improvement should be even more apparent in this light. In that place, communication can be preserved and lead to understanding. In that place, each group can be reminded that the other group still has the same hopes and fears about the success of the enterprise they share.

Another key difference between the two sides of the diagram has to do with the types of data they produce and the treatment of the data, especially by management. The data produced by innovators is a representation of ideas. Each of those ideas must compete to get into the world of implementation, where, as we have just discussed, resources are limited and not every idea can be implemented. Also, some ideas just simply *should* not be implemented. Thus some screening method must be applied to these ideas. To some degree, data may be used to validate the advisability of an idea. Highly innovative ideas especially, however, may have little in the current real world to help validate them. In some cases, such as process improvement projects, there may be multiple solutions that seem likely or practically guaranteed to achieve desired results, and some subjective judgment may be required to choose the "best" solution. "Best" may be a relative term in such cases. The "best" choice may not be the most obvious choice or the one best validated by data but might instead be the one which best motivates stakeholders to support and carry out the required actions. Choices made about deployment, no matter how carefully they are studied, are an attempt to some extent to predict the future. They may not involve anything that can really be called a solution but must instead be called simply a choice. One reason for this lack of assuredness is that these predictive choices must be made, not by identifying a clear theoretical path, but by attempting to find the best balance in the predicted effects of several factors. All of this means that decisions about which paths of innovation to pursue will almost always be made in a bit of a logical haze. To a significant degree, arbitrary, subjective, and/or assumptive judgment must be applied to innovative ideas and to deployment data in general, and it is important to note that such judgment will reflect primarily on the intellectual and/or imaginative capabilities of the innovators. An appropriate summary of this logic would be that deployment data produces assumptions which must be subjected to judgment.

Application data is another matter altogether. There is no grand idea or scheme behind such data. It is simply the empirical result of observation. The only matters open to judgment with regard to application data are whether appropriate sampling techniques were used or whether there is any reason to suspect "spin" or outright falsification of the data. Sampling errors may result in failure to collect data that correctly represent the process or phenomenon under observation. Spin and data falsification attempt to do the same, but they add motive. I hope that the former is a more common problem than the latter in your organization. If the latter is a common problem, however, an obvious question would be why conditions in the organization would provide motive—more on this later. At any rate, I will discount spin and falsification for two reasons: first, as I have already noted, they are likely to be symptoms of the organization's health as opposed to the process under observation; second, even if there is reason to suspect the data in its delivered state, the raw data is probably still available and will still provide accurate information when subjected to appropriate analysis. One point of motive must remain under discussion, however, and that is the fact that application data represents the ability of organizations and individuals to actually perform—to do things. When we judge the quality of ideas coming from innovation, that judgment is much less threatening than judgment applied to application data. After all, we are apt to be less harsh in judging one's ability to imagine as opposed to one's ability to do. Therefore, the tools that we use to judge data coming from application should be stripped of assumption and any hint of arbitrariness. In fact, we should not "judge" application data at all; we should analyze it and use it objectively to identify where and how to improve. (This does not absolve poor performers from judgment; if correct analysis of the data unequivocally shows the root cause of poor performance to be a person or persons, then improvement may mean counseling, warning, or firing those so indicated. In an organization where this process is carried out fairly and humanely, there should be little reason to fear that such actions will lead to adverse effects on future data.) The summary of all this logic is that application data produces facts that must be subjected to analysis.

An important distinction needs to be made between actions and motives, and one must always be careful to keep that distinction in mind as it relates to learning. I remember an organization I used to work with that used training (or attempted to) as a corrective action for failure. When tasks were incorrectly performed, the offenders were routinely sent to the Training department for recertification. There is some surface logic to this, but it ignores the aspect of motivation. I could tell that, in most cases, the people being recertified had usually just been caught doing something to short-cut a process. They had known what they were doing, but they were motivated, perhaps because they wanted to show productivity or because of a simple desire to be more comfortable, to act contrary to instructions. One day, somebody told me something that helped me see why this approach was fundamentally flawed. This person said to me, "You know, if you hold a gun to their head and they can do it right, *it's not a training issue.*" I have treasured this principle ever since. Training is practically powerless to change motive. When people exhibit behavior that is contradictory to policy and procedure, one is well advised to consider whether the system around them gives them reason to do so. The question that must be asked is whether their behavior was a matter of ignorance or choice. If the system effectively encourages behavior outside the desired norms, then the system—or at least the measurement of system performance—is usually the root cause of the behavior.

There is a hugely important footnote to this talk about application data, and it has to do with data that reflects failure. Failure is embarrassing. Failure is painful. Failure is cause for fear, perhaps terror if consequences for failure are known to be severe. Failure is also inevitable, at least at some level. Somewhere, somehow, every organization will do something that doesn't completely measure up to expectations. If the system for supplying application data works impartially, though, it will be reported like all other factors of performance. Because of the views of failure described above, however, organizations may employ some form of denial to avoid confronting failure. They may downplay it or ignore it altogether. They may blame it on a person or persons and thus absolve the organization, the process, and/or the product of any blame. If they take any of these paths, though, it is certain they will not learn much from it. Few organizational cultures reinforce, much less reward, the ability to identify and admit to failure or weakness of any kind. Identifying and admitting to such weakness, though, is a critical first step to identifying the areas that must logically offer the most room for and benefit from improvement, since they are the current source of less-than-optimal performance.

I don't know about you, but failure has taught me some of my most important lessons. It's not my favorite way to learn, but it is effective. That learning never came, though, until I admitted, confronted, and analyzed the failure in order to determine its root cause and correct that root. I have seen few organizations capable of consistently managing failure productively. I have been witness to the shooting of many messengers of failure, however, and I have concluded that no factor leads more to deception in application data than the *justified* fear of bearing bad news. It is easy and comforting to blame a few to avoid embarrassment of the many, but all too often the many bear a portion (if not most) of the real blame and have a lot to learn from the failure at hand. This point will come up again later in the book in more detail, but it was at this point in the development of the model that I first realized the impact of this particular learning blindness, so I feel obliged to introduce it here.

I would like to discuss one last thing before I end this chapter: the range of applicability of this model. Most of my discussion up to this point has focused on how this model applies in large organizations, where one group designs and another produces—in my particular paradigm, I had product design and manufacturing in mind. Indeed, describing the interaction of those two groups is what I set out to do when I first started creating the model. When I got it to this point, however, I took a second look at it and found that its applicability was deeper and more varied than that. Besides just describing the interaction between groups of people devoted to innovating and groups devoted to implementing, it stands up to scrutiny as a model to describe the *interaction* between innovation and implementation, *wherever* that interaction occurs. Within large organizations, that may go much further than just design and production. As I mentioned above, this model might be applied to the customer/supplier interaction. Human relations groups develop policies that must be implemented by many organizations—which might put a design group in an implementing role with regard to the model. Quality groups may develop data and processes that ensure a competitive advantage for their company; these must be implemented and used to advantage by sales and marketing. Within a manufacturing group, process engineers create equipment improvements to be delivered to production. Production teams come up with ideas which they themselves must execute, so that they serve the function of both innovator and implementer, not as separate groups but as different phases or facets of the same group. In the same context, a design group might decide on a way to improve the quality of the design packages they deliver, and focus on their function as implementers of a package creation process.

As I broke this down to smaller and smaller groups, I found that even groups were not necessary for this model to work, because I found it working in my own head. I imagine things which I then must decide to do or not do. I submit designs to myself which my own judgment reviews for practicality and/or profit; some I reject, some I accept and carry out. I review my "application data"—my actions, my performance, my success, my failure—to decide how I shall change my behavior in the future to be more efficient, more successful, or just more of the person I hope will be remembered by others. I have learned the value of that safe place, supported by data, where I can objectively apply the best of my thinking and the results of my doing. In short, this model seems to apply everywhere that learning and improvement happen, and the more I study the model, the more I understand and believe that life can be better.

Reflection:

- This book only provides you with an Engine and a chassis; you are responsible for the rest of your vehicle.

    - Finish the vehicle design—at least in your mind. Picture your organization, with its unique values, mission, and resources, running with this Engine under the hood.

- Learning is an interaction between innovation and implementation.

    - Who are the innovators in your organization? The implementers? Think about them in the context of this model. Any insights?
    - What is the quality of interaction between your innovators and implementers? Do you see "over the wall syndrome" there?
    - How well is the process for delivering deployment data defined? How well is the process for delivering application data <u>as a learning tool</u> defined?

- Improvement benefits from a "safe" place, supported by data, where innovators and implementers can learn together.

    - Does your organization have such a place (i.e., do you have trustworthy, objective processes for looking at what's new and what you have done and learning from both)?
    - Is mutual respect expected, modeled, and reinforced in your organization?

- Application data benefits from analysis; deployment data is subject to judgment.

    - How comfortable are you with the subjective nature of "best" choices about innovation? Would you overturn a deployment choice if you found that a seemingly less logical choice would be better supported—and therefore probably more successfully implemented—by those involved in the process?
    - Does your organization use reliable, statistical methods for defining data collection plans and analyzing the resulting data?

- There is a tremendous amount to be learned from failure.

  - Does your own experience validate this? What are some failures (or at least some things you could have done better) in your life from which you have gained significant wisdom?
  - How good are you at identifying and confronting your own weaknesses and/or failures?
  - What level of "messenger shooting" does your organization experience? What is the impact on learning, as this book uses that term?
  - Does your organization have a systematic process for examining itself for weaknesses and failures and learning from them without blame?

Chapter 5

What to Do (Part 1)

"If we don't change direction soon, we'll end up where we're going."

<u>Professor Irwin Corey</u>

So far, I have dealt mostly with equations and diagrams. I think I have introduced enough theory and background at this point, however, to move on to where some rubber meets some road (an apt phrase in light of the car/engine metaphor adopted in the last chapter). Let's take a break from theory and models—the left side of the Engine, as you should now be thinking—and move on to behavior and action (the right side of the model). I would like to talk for a bit specifically about *what to do* and *how to do it*, in the light of our current understanding of these equations and diagrams. I say "current understanding" because, since I have not completed the construction of the Engine, there are still some bits missing that will be needed for complete comprehension. Note that the chapter title identifies this as "Part 1"; there will be a later chapter—"What to Do (Part 2)," if you hadn't guessed—that will return to these specifics after we finish adding all the parts to the Engine. In fact, I will rehearse again in that chapter some of the things I am bringing up in this one—with the added functionality of the completed Engine as new context. Also, I will devote yet another later chapter specifically to what leaders must do in light of these concepts to optimize organizational learning and improvement, and thus, success. Many of the things I will advise you to do can be found in the work of other authors. Some are just standard procedure for those who have studied adult learning. My hope is that the Engine will give you an easy way to remember <u>why</u> to do those things. In fact, with the Engine as inspiration you could have figured them all out yourself. You certainly know enough right now, though, to be able to take specific steps toward adapting this Engine and these principles to your own organization. Here's how.

- *Take an aggressive stance toward change.*

Change is the energy from which you will derive success. Every time change takes you by surprise, or at the end of a long battle against your resistance to it, you will lose the opportunity to take advantage of its energy to power your progress. As an illustration, I will use an example that almost suffers from being a cliché these days: the failure of American automobile manufacturers in the 1970's to anticipate, acknowledge, or take advantage of the public's shifting expectations. I hope American auto manufacturing companies will forgive me for dragging this poor old horse out for what may be perceived as one more beating, and I apologize for what they may see as another embarrassing reflection on old news. The truth is, though, that the scope of this example and its familiarity to so many people now in the heart of their career lives make it a lesson from which there is still much to be learned.

In the 1970's fuel prices and the beginnings of improved consumer awareness let Japanese imports gain a foothold in the American market. The more the American public saw of the Japanese imports, the more they wanted cars that were smaller, sportier, more fuel-efficient, more reliable, etc. It wasn't as if the American companies couldn't have foreseen this; in fact, there is evidence they did. Ford, at least, saw the desire of Americans for something along these lines as early as the mid-1950's; the result was the Thunderbird. The first few years saw the Thunderbird as an American sports car: small, agile, and nicely powerful. By the 60's, though, the Thunderbird was well on its transitional path to being just another full-sized sedan amid a flock of similar competitors. For one thing, Ford had failed to realize the value of a niche market car. They wanted to make it as big a seller as possible, and that meant making it . . . well, just like everything else. In the early 60's they again came out with a car designed to appeal to that same niche market: the Mustang. Again they tried to increase its general market appeal at the expense of the original intent, and by the end of the 60's the Mustang was bigger and less distinct from its competitors (not sedans this time, but the big "muscle cars" of the late 60's and early 70's). Both of these efforts, however, make clear the fact that Ford had seen the appeal of smaller, sportier cars—to a smaller, distinct market. Among the things they did *not* see—beyond just the market for smaller cars—was their opportunity to start marketing to diverse consumer segments. Their idea of market segments at the time would seem to have been based almost exclusively on price. At the heart of their assumptions seemed to be a belief that everybody *really* wanted a Cadillac or a Lincoln, and that other models needed to exist in order to allow those who could not afford the best to have something that seemed a reasonable compromise. They also did not foresee the desire for fuel economy that the 70's would bring, nor did they react well to it. When the public, driven by need if not desire to try a smaller automobile of non-domestic manufacture, realized how little American manufacturers had done in comparison to address the reliability of their products, many felt downright betrayed. Their "own" companies had not, it suddenly seemed, had their best interests in mind. The phrase "planned obsolescence" came into the public lexicon at this time and seemed to exemplify the callous disregard for the consumer that too many companies had taken as their entitlement. American auto manufacturers would take years to recover from this simple failure to anticipate or even react to change. In some ways, perhaps, it never has recovered or will, as non-domestic auto manufacturers now seem to be a significant and permanent part of the landscape.

There are, right now as I write this, dozens, hundreds, perhaps thousands of similar scenarios spinning their way to fruition. As an example, I might point to the publishing industry itself. In the 70's, as people began to make cassette tape copies of their favorite albums, and certainly in the 80's when people started to copy files from personal computer to disk, it might have easily been foreseen that the existing structures of publishing rights and royalties would be threatened. A quarter of a century later, however, Napster seemed to come as a complete surprise to the publishing industry, and to date I have heard few really creative ways to adapt publishing structures to the realities of digital information exchange.

What changes are happening in your area of endeavor? In the national mindset about what you do? In the character of your company itself, as it ages, grows or diminishes, becomes more diverse, becomes more globally affected or involved? How are you reacting to those changes? I can just about promise you that you are playing the ostrich with at least some of those changes; our natural resistance to change almost demands it. How, specifically, can you work to keep as much of your head as possible out of the sand and focused on the onslaught of change? Here are some ways:

- Engage as many of your organization's intellectual resources as possible, at all levels, to identify oncoming change and ways to take advantage of it. This means going beyond the "suggestion box" level. It means holding periodic workshops with structured participation from a broad mix of stakeholders.

- Ensure that your organization is well-versed in the techniques and philosophies of continuous improvement. By continually implementing incremental improvements and fostering a culture that promotes that mindset, you are likely to leave yourself less of a leap to make when external circumstances force relatively sudden, dramatic levels of change.

- Use some portion of your organization's best intellectual resources to conduct "war games" around some of the most adventurous and the most threatening possibilities. The wildest of ideas are usually capable of being domesticated and, with imagination, turned to the practical pursuit of Progress.

• *Change your perspective about what you think of as "communication"—it may be unidentified learning.*

If you have worked in a large corporation for any significant period, you have probably seen or heard the results of some survey or another about employee perceptions within the company. I have seen several over the years, and my experience tells me that if there is one aspect of any corporation that employees always perceive as needing improvement, it is communication. No matter what the condition of the company or its level of morale, employees always seem to say that improved communication is among the top few things the company could use to achieve a higher level of success.

What they are really saying—in a way you need to train yourself to hear—is that the company doesn't learn as effectively as it could. That statement implies a logical connection between communication and learning; I have already made that connection implicit in the equation:

Learning = Communication + Application

Communication that does not result in learning is almost meaningless, if you think about it—sort of like raw data, requiring analysis to turn it into information that can then be useful in driving decisions. Application of what has been communicated must occur for any meaning to be derived. Behavior must change as a result of the new information, or at least mindsets must be changed so that new conclusions may be reached. Even in repetitive processes, we often must "communicate" (learn) exactly how the next cycle of the process should run. Even the most mechanical processes can be seen as a chain of Engines, with each activity in the process generating an output that must then be correctly understood and used by some receiving activity. If the current cycle involves different materials or a different customer, those changes must be "learned." Since all of this is driving Productivity (in the Engine's

3rd dimension), it can soon be seen that Improvement and Productivity both depend substantially on the speedy, accurate, and motivational "communication" of information.

I have covered some of this logic already, but do you really realize how deeply this concept drives? When you do something as simple as scheduling lunch with another person, *learning* must happen. Your lunch partner must *learn* the location and the time of the lunch, probably executing some behavior (like marking a calendar) to solidify that learning. I make this trivial example to make what I hope is a profound point; you have probably never truly seen or even imagined how much learning is happening in your organization. All of the training we undertake by design is only the tip of a massive iceberg, the rest of the iceberg being concealed under our almost dismissive use of the term "communication." Our concept of the word "communication" and its importance in pursuit of success has, I think, been blunted by the obvious and continual failures we see in communication every day. Errors in communication, being so common, are thus taken somewhat for granted and come to be expected. (By the way, doesn't that sound a lot like the way we looked at quality just a few decades ago? *A certain number of defective parts has to be expected . . .*)

The same cannot be said for the word "teaching." If we are tasked to "teach" a new procedure, we take a different level of diligence to that task than if we had been tasked merely to "communicate" that procedure. "Communicating" the procedure can be interpreted as merely sending the party involved a written copy. "Teaching" requires that we make sure that party really understands the new information and is able to make decisions and act in accordance with that understanding. "Teaching" implies a whole new level of responsibility above merely "communicating." The communicator must bear the responsibility for ensuring the accuracy of communication, for only he or she knows the original information in its original form and is thus the only one who can confirm whether the knowledge has been accurately and completely transferred. Despite this obvious logic, I have often seen receivers get the blame for mistakes, the assumption being that their failure to "get it" was through inattention or incompetence.

It is certainly true that almost all communication can benefit from being perceived as learning. It is also true that realizing this can be a bit overwhelming and could even prompt one to over-react. Like a microscope revealing microbes in your tap water, this new insight on communication suddenly reveals untold thousands or even millions of learning opportunities in your organization going forward without oversight or accountability. The value, though, is more in the microscope itself than in any attempt to gain individual control over all the microbes. Learn to look at every bit of communication as learning. Establish for yourself at what level action should be taken on that insight. You will gradually make "seeing" learning and improvement an instinct. First practice consciously, and then continue until unconscious competence (instinct?) is attained. Then decide how much to let this instinct affect you.

What actions can you take on this? Here are a few:

- Change your own mindset. Assimilate this information now. From this point henceforth, take at least a moment to consider every exchange of information that occurs around you as a potential learning event. Consider the consequences of failure if the information is misunderstood or corrupted. Take action where potential benefits or risks are high.

- Set a personal example by taking an extra measure of "teaching" responsibility for information you deliver. Make sure your receiver "gets it"—understands not only what you said, but why you said it and what they should do or think about as a result of having heard it.

- Ask more pointed questions when people in meetings talk about communication being a problem. Ask questions that will reveal whether learning is impaired as a result of such problems and how much that impairment may jeopardize the effort at hand.

• *Become an expert at identifying your own and your organization's soft spots.*

Call them weaknesses, vulnerabilities, or opportunities for improvement; they are the "soft spots" in your capability to perform. At least at first, this is not a skill which is likely either to be easy or to make you popular. Identifying the less-than-optimal characteristics of others has predictable risks. Identifying your own is painful, especially if you go beyond the superficial. The need is obvious, however, and not only must you identify them, you must positively confront them. Where you or your organization lacks required skills (weakness), you are the least efficient. Where you or your organization is least prepared for change (vulnerability), you risk being blind-sided. Where you or your organization runs a high defect rate (opportunity for improvement)— even if that rate is "acceptable" or "within industry norms"—you invite competition. Finally, it should be blindingly obvious from the simple standpoint of the Pareto principle that your greatest opportunity to improve lies in the things you do worst.

What you need to do here is also blindingly obvious, but, as I said, it is far from easy:

- Be completely honest with yourself and others about capabilities. This will mean confronting others with what are probably some of their least favorite topics. Learn to do this in a way that maintains their self-respect and attaches no blame. Learn to do the same for yourself. Learn communication skills that allow you to talk about soft spots without implying that they are the result of personal or professional incompetence. Use some of the other techniques in this chapter to plan learning that will address the needs.

- *Understand learning—in the broad definition of this model— as a critical factor in the cycle time of improvement. Adjust your expectations accordingly.*

The Improvement Engine is more than a model for improvement; it is a model for execution. The model assumes that improvement will be built into execution because of the natural human tendency to learn from experience. Learning, therefore, should be expected as part of the normal cycle time of execution, and if any improvement is intentionally sought, learning may become a significant or even the primary component of that cycle time.

Some of my best examples of what happens when this point is ignored or forgotten come from the implementation of major software/automation programs and efforts intended to achieve cultural change. Most of the failures can be traced to the assumption that providing training— or worse yet, "communicating the change"—ensures learning. In the case of the software/automation projects, there tends to be a focus on the installation and programming activities, and a tendency to try to package the necessary learning into efficient deliveries (e.g., classroom training—the discussions under the next item point out the hazards of depending on classroom training). The cultural change efforts tend to suffer from a sort of small delusion that seems to be self-generating in the natural course of such programs: a confidence that people will believe that the organization will change in the manner described. The real effect in both cases is the same; people do not learn or change their behavior as fast as predicted, and the implementation over-runs the learning. For software/automation projects, this usually means significant unplanned follow-up training, often in coaching mode with individuals having particular problems. This last bit of learning is often done under pressure, first because it was not planned and is therefore poorly perceived, and second because actual use of the system, once the system has been fully installed, becomes a real impact on people's ability to get work done. For cultural change projects, this usually means watching the program disappear over the "philosophy *du jour*" horizon, usually to a chorus of "I told you so," delivered with shaking heads and folded arms.

The problem in such cases is a simple one; in both cases, the cycle time of delivering the product was out of synch with the ability of the organization to receive the product. Although these two types of projects may seem worlds apart, they share a critical common point; they depend on the ability of their customer to translate existing behavior into a new model. In the case of software/automation, people who may have used forms and interpersonal communication to accomplish a set of tasks now find themselves facing a keyboard and a sometimes bewildering multitude of data entry and reporting screens. In the case of cultural change projects, they are told one day—usually in a class or communication meeting—that old standards of behavior are out; they are now expected to act differently. Often accepting this difference requires a good bit of faith that the organization will, in fact, value this new type of behavior. (After all, this is a culture *change*; that means the new behavior is not currently in evidence. The logical assumption is that it is not in evidence because it was not previously valued.) Predictably, real conditions in the workplace the next day are not significantly different, nor are they a month later. The training and/or communication events have been checked off the project list, the arms have folded, and the heads have shaken; pretty soon nobody even wears the T-shirt (<u>unless</u> there is an observable change in the behavior of organizational leaders that matches the stated expectations of the change effort—I will have more to say on this after the Engine is complete and even more when I talk about the responsibilities of leaders).

Sometimes people just need time to change, and sometimes time needs to be devoted to convincing them that change is really expected and will be rewarded. I think of it as time needed for gestation and acceptance. When the schedule for such projects is created, it is easy to underestimate or forget this time altogether. Even if any such time is built into the schedule, if that schedule should come under any pressure from management (and what schedule doesn't?), it is the most difficult time to justify and the most likely to be compressed.

All of the above relates to how learning can lengthen cycle times. Just as importantly, learning can shorten them. In project plans we tend to focus on activities required. In a project devoted to improvement, since improvement requires learning and improvement, this means we tend to concentrate on the change portion. In projects devoted to execution, we tend to forget that the communication events in that project are learning events as well. In both cases, singling learning out for attention can have significant cycle time benefits. My own experience tells me that where activities on a project are late or not to specification, a failure in learning (often in its disguise as "communication") is usually more to blame than any actual incapability to produce the expected result. There is data (I'll talk specifically about it in Chapter 7) to show that decisions made and implemented by groups of stakeholders have a shorter cycle time than the same decisions made and implemented by individuals. One of the primary reasons for this difference is the increased communication—and thus learning—resulting from the group's involvement.

By focusing on learning, you can have a positive effect on cycle time in one of two ways. First, by designing an effective learning strategy for each project—see specific hints below on this topic as well as others in this chapter—you can decrease the time required to complete the project and reduce rework, remediation, and error elimination time at the end of the project. Second, devoting attention to learning can allow you to achieve a greater level of improvement from a given level of activity. The cycle time of the activity itself may not be affected, but you will have shortened the time required to gain a similar amount of wisdom. Whether you affect the pace of activity or the pace of learning, both are reductions to the cycle time of improvement.

Specifically, do the following:

- Examine projects critically for how much change they require. Especially where they require change in mental models (e.g., software/automation) or change in attitudes/values (cultural change), build in time for gestation and acceptance, or start the communication/learning processes earlier than you might originally be inclined. Defend the need for this time.

- Especially with long term, complex, or mission-critical projects, consider building in learning "checkpoints." These are points in the project where the organization's success in assimilating the required learning and behavior changes is measured before progressing. If the project is outstripping the organization's ability to learn, either slow the project or take action to increase the pace of learning.

- Most people tend to think of training as an activity that slows down execution. If you have any tendency to believe that, change your mindset. Well-designed learning speeds execution.

- ***Don't use a "course catalog" approach to training. Design appropriate learning strategies for each specific need.***

An organization I once worked for required a certain portion of all employees' time be spent in training. The company was fairly large and had a training department that offered many classes with in-house instruction and scheduled regular offerings of some topics through hired instructors. The training department published a catalog of courses offered. Here's a fairly typical scenario for how that training was planned. As part of a periodic process (quarterly goals review, annual performance review, etc.), employee and supervisor looked at the employee's capabilities and considered how they might expand to allow the employee to be more versatile or learn skills that might lead to promotion. If the learning required was tied to a specific company procedure within the control of the department, cross-training was arranged with an experienced individual. If a more generic capability was needed (use of a software package, improved interpersonal skills, meeting facilitation, etc.), the employee was scheduled to take a class on the subject. In cases where specific connections could not be established between new capabilities and new types of work, the employee and supervisor would peruse the catalog for—or the employee might suggest—existing classes which might be useful.

Now, depending on where you are, this might sound fairly normal, or it might even sound like a progressive learning paradise. I remember folks from other companies commenting that our requirement for training was enviable, especially since it put some responsibility on management to make time for training. Our access to in-house learning also seemed marvelous to some other organizations. The truth of the matter, however, was that almost all the identifiable benefit from this approach came from cross-training: people being taught specific skills, usually on the job, to make them more flexible in their ability to take on multiple tasks in their work area. This training was almost always conducted with some sort of appropriate preparation and follow-up (as discussed below), and there was usually immediate expectation that such cross-training would be used in the workplace. The classroom training, since it seldom had appropriate preparation or follow-up, became privately acknowledged as more of a morale booster than a critical learning process.

There are more ways to learn than in a classroom. Classroom training is driven—and limited—by the instructor's ability to teach, not the participant's desire to learn. An instructor must design a course that covers the needs of many in order to be cost-effective. This fact alone demands that each specific student's needs will not be optimally met. Additionally, most classroom training simply delivers more information than a student can effectively remember long enough to put the learning into practice. There are options to the classroom. Coaching, mentoring, self-paced learning programs, and cross-training with colleagues are the most obvious alternatives, and combinations may be derived from any of these approaches.

The point here is that learning deserves a good design, and one-size-fits-all is seldom optimal. By now, I would hope that I have convinced you that learning is not a topic to be taken lightly. If you are going to be serious about learning, then take time and be creative in planning it. Let your annual goals and your project plans drive your learning needs, not a browse through a course catalog. Once those needs are identified, question those who must learn about the ways they learn best (including yourself). Some may say that classroom training works very well for them; by all means use it as a tool for those people. If another strategy is more effective with a particular individual, try to find a way for that person to gain the learning in the mode that he or she believes works best. If you are the learner, ask for the same consideration. Do not let the deceptive efficiency of classroom training lure you away from more effective methods. Do not let an arbitrary inner demand for consistency prevent you from using entirely different methods to teach two separate people the same thing.

Do not overlook the complexity involved in learning even fairly straightforward business tools if they involve changing people. The best project management software and consummate user skills are not enough to properly outfit a successful project manager, for instance. That person must also manage changing and teaching the people involved and interested in the project. Success will involve understanding and balancing multiple concerns, navigating internal politics, making effective use of internal systems, etc. Classroom training may have taught the learner how to manipulate the tool; they know how to "read the map" of the territory they will have to navigate. I strongly recommend that, in the case of learning involving similarly complex skills, mentoring be used as an <u>immediate</u> follow-on. If training teaches you how to read the map, mentoring enables you to know the territory. Any travelling salesperson knows the difference.

I have already identified most of the actions you can take on learning designs within the body of the discussion, but I will highlight the key items:

- Get familiar with training methods other than classroom training. Find out which methods work best with individuals within your organization. When learning needs are identified for them, use those methods.

- Identify learning needs before you look for course offerings. (I know this may seem obvious, but I can't help remembering watching people looking through the catalog and identifying this year's training with the "I haven't taken this yet" method.)

- Think of classroom training in general as a supplementary action, perhaps 25% of the effort required to drive learning. The real learning will depend more on good preparation and follow-up, as discussed below. Strongly consider mentoring as a major learning strategy for your organization.

- Put the identification of learning needs and the design of learning strategies at a higher priority and devote more time to it. If you are not convinced that these activities deserve this, then read chapters 1 through 4 again.

- ***Keep a critical eye on the flow of new and theoretical knowledge.***

This is one of those swamps you are likely to forget about draining after a day of battling alligators. New and theoretical knowledge is the herald of change to come, and we have already discussed the natural resistance to change—and how to be aggressive in that arena. Actually, this might have been listed as one of the actions to take in order to be aggressive toward change; I considered the topic significant enough, however, to deserve some attention of its own.

By "keeping a critical eye" on the flow of knowledge, I do not mean managing that entire flow personally. Especially in these post-information-explosion, ultra-specialized days, there is just too much to know about any business for one person to be able to keep track of new, relevant knowledge. My best advice here is to build the flow into your culture. Make sure that everybody knows that gathering, synthesizing, and communicating new knowledge are tasks valued by the organization.

You personally have a responsibility to contribute to the flow, of course. Here's how you can do that:

- Read journals that talk about what's new in your fields. Find relevant Internet sites and visit them periodically. Keep in touch with others who do what you do and exchange thoughts. (Most people do something like this. Here comes the kicker, however.)

- Synthesize what you learn. Learn to state it concisely, as a conversation starter. Identify connections with other people's fields of interest. Then share what you learn with your boss, colleagues, employees, etc. (This may be more difficult— much more difficult—in some organizations than others; if your organization makes this hard to do, see below.) Be a good example at bringing new knowledge into your organization in an efficient, interesting, relevant manner.

I'll come back to this more when I talk about leadership responsibilities, but here are some things an organization can do to ensure the flow of new ideas:

- Hire proven learners. By this I do not mean to restrict hiring to higher levels of education. I mean first of all to hire those who are driven to learn. Formal education is certainly a possible indicator here, but personal and professional experience may be just as strong. Design interview questions to identify people who have managed significant and/or multiple personal changes in order to accomplish goals.

- Ensure that your leaders are exemplary learners. I'll save discussion on this 'til later.

- Make teaching a recognized part of everyone's job. Do not let your organization become one where hoarding knowledge and information is a way of building power or influence. Reward those who make others more capable by sharing what they know. Make this expectation clear from the first interview with a prospective employee/member.

- Encourage forums—but ask them for results. Create opportunities for relevant special-interest groups to gather in your organization and—to the extent that confidentialities are not likely to be jeopardized—in league with other organizations who share that interest. Especially if the groups are internal, ask them for results; give them questions to research and scenarios to explore. Get periodic reports from internal groups and from the representatives to outside groups about what has been learned and how to disseminate that learning appropriately.

• ***Ensure appropriate preparation for training and follow-up after training.***

(*Please . . . even if you don't actually do any of the other things I advise in this chapter, at least take my advice on this point. These two actions are relatively easy and will dramatically increase the value you get from any training.*)

I have taught a lot of classes in workplace environments. I don't know the exact number, but I'm pretty sure it's into four figures. In almost every class I have taught, there has been at least one person who really had no idea specifically why he or she was there. The reasons they give *sound* like real reasons: "My supervisor said I should take this class."

(Translation: "I don't think I need this and I don't want to be here, but my boss made me.") "This is on the list of required classes for the position I want." (Translation: "I don't see why I need this and I don't want to be here, but I need it to get the job I really want.") "I needed four hours to make my quarterly training requirement." (Translation: Oh, there is no translation. That's as real a reason as there is. It's just depressing to be part of such a waste.)

I'm not going to beat around the bush here. <u>There is no excuse for this</u>, and the primary responsibility for allowing it—or preventing it—is in leadership's hands, be that a manager, supervisor, executive, or even a parent with a school-age child. If you send people to learn things, you owe it to them to tell them why.

Learning is too important to waste, as I hope I have made abundantly clear so far. The most critical step in not wasting it is to make sure that learners know *why* they are learning. What condition demands that they learn? Are procedures changing? Do they need to be more versatile within their group's area of responsibilities? Do they need these skills to do their existing job better? Are they expected to be more productive or produce higher quality work armed with these skills? Are they learning these skills to prepare for possible promotion? If so, how will these skills be used in that position? Perhaps most important, how and when, *specifically*, will they be able to practice these skills after they are learned? As you might note, the only person qualified to answer these questions (especially the last one) for a specific employee is the person to whom that employee reports directly.

The answers to these questions provide motivation. That motivation will drive participants to actively engage with the learning process. They will ask questions during the learning process to ensure that they understand the relation between the current discussion or activity and their work. They might even be more critical and demanding of the training, and for the most part, that's probably a good thing; I've seen way too many mediocre learning events get rave reviews simply because, since there was no expectation of really using the new knowledge or skills, there was no reason to be dissatisfied.

Just as disappointing as the unprepared learner is the unapplied learner. By this I mean the person who put time and effort into gaining new knowledge and/or skills which were then left to wither since they were never applied.

I will continue my effort not to beat around the bush. There is no excuse for this, and the primary responsibility for allowing it—or preventing it—is in leadership's hands. (I will cut parents a little slack on this one. Kids learn too much every day to try to make sure that every bit of it is then used in real life. A little slack is not a free ride, however. If they want their kids to enjoy school and learning, parents need to know what their kids are learning and help show its context in real life.)

Especially in the case of classroom training, new learning is a fragile and temporary thing. If it is not immediately reinforced by being used, it will disappear. By the end of one week, approximately 50% of learning that has not been reinforced or applied will disappear. By the end of two weeks, that number will increase to 70%—90%. There is a simple remedy, however; make sure that when you plan training, you also plan for opportunities to use that training immediately. If the skills require experience to build them to a truly effective level, make sure that initial assignments to use the new learning are fairly simple; if possible (or necessary), create opportunities to practice where mistakes or failure can be accepted. Do your best to ensure success the first few times the new learning is put to task; then gradually raise expectations. Continue follow-up until proficiency reaches at least a minimally acceptable level for normal use of those skills in the workplace.

One of the reasons this seemingly simple bit of communication may be difficult is that it may involve one of the earlier and more difficult points in this chapter: identifying soft spots. Almost anything a person needs to learn might be considered a soft spot, and, depending on how sensitive a soft spot, may respond poorly to confrontation. In the best scenarios, you are telling somebody to go learn something to which they have had little exposure and which clearly relates to new work requirements, predictable performance improvement, or preparation for advancement. A slightly more difficult scenario arises when you assign learning which the assignee does not see as relevant to performance in his or her organizational role. In effect, this person believes that the proposed learning is "not part of my job," and this may be cause for some tension or confrontation. Probably the worst-case scenario involves having to tell a person to learn something which he believes he already does well. The underlying text here is that your perception of current performance is inadequate, despite this person's contrary perceptions. The opportunity is ripe for emotional awkwardness.

The last two scenarios may indeed have some of the natural hazards of soft spot identification in them. Such hazards must not dissuade you, however. Preparing for and following up on assigned learning are vital to effective learning.

The actions here are a bit redundant, but they bear repeating:

- If you assign people to train, make sure they know what they are learning and why. In particular, set a plan for how and when they will use the new skills in the workplace. If you are the learner and this is not done for you, ask for it.

- Execute the post-learning plan. Make sure that new skills are used within hours or, at most, a few days of their having been learned. Start with basic use in a low-risk setting if possible. Especially if the skills are complex, consider if mentoring is recommended.

- ***Examine processes, projects, and strategies for information hand-offs—identify them as separate learning actions, and use this model to plan them.***

Now that you are looking at "communication" a little differently, apply that perspective to planning and improvement. In every project and process, there is information that must pass from one organization to another, from one individual to another, from one activity to another, etc. Next time you create a detailed project plan or (re)design a process, build in specific steps to identify and review such points. Using your changed perspective of "communication," regard them as learning points. Remember that the "bottom line" of each of these events is what is learned, not what is communicated. Where the success of information exchange is critical, and especially if history suggests there is risk of failure, spend some more time planning actions to reduce that risk. Ask yourself some of the other questions that we have already covered in this chapter. How much real change does the project introduce? Is "convincing time" required for attitudes to shift? What is the best way, in each learning event, to structure that learning; is coaching required? What can be done as part of the project plan to prepare and follow-up on training? Especially in existing processes, what information must be communicated, how must it be interpreted, how must it be applied?

Here's how to do this:

- Use your normal procedures to generate a rough draft of the actions necessary to complete the project. (I'm assuming you have procedures; if you want to know how to use the most effective group process to accomplish this, read Dennis Romig's discussion of action planning in <u>Breakthrough Teamwork</u>.) Review that draft for places where "communication" is required (or worse, assumed), remembering that communication is not the object; learning is. Identify these points for further examination.
- Examine each of the identified points in light of your new perspectives on the importance of and actions necessary to successful learning. Give consideration to the consequences of failure, and apply due diligence to ensuring success, especially in cases where risk is high.

- Use the above review to identify new project actions and/or measures.
- Keep this perspective in mind through execution of the project. Modify or add learning steps if you see opportunity. Review execution of planned actions to see if learning was effective; be prepared to change techniques if data shows otherwise.
- Make sure that, wherever one group is expected to implement another's decisions, there is early and frequent interaction. This simply gets the whole Engine turning early and quickly; it decreases response time, time to market, etc.

- ### *Conduct "pre-learning" exercises before major projects.*

I once worked for a group which was about to undertake a huge project. The project had a lot to do with the company's future, and budget was equal to about a quarter of the entire company's annual revenue. It was the sort of project this group was accustomed to being involved in about every three to five years.

I was asked to facilitate project planning, with special attention to learning issues. I began by asking several individuals in the immediate group who had significant experience in similar previous projects two basic questions: "What has historically been less-than-optimal in projects of this nature?" and, "Who else has been involved in these projects?" These questions served the purposes of identifying the areas probably most in need of attention in the upcoming project (the best opportunities, for the optimistic among you) and identifying an expanded network of people with whom communication would be required and who had more ideas on where to do better this time. An important reason for identifying chronic problem areas is that if they are chronic, they are likely to be systematic and may thus require attention from a process improvement standpoint *before* the project begins, or at least a lot earlier than has been the history in previous projects. The lesson here is to identify your soft spots early, since they will need the most work and will benefit the most from that work.

In the course of this questioning, I was talking to a project veteran one day, and he told me I ought to take a look at some of the "lessons learned" documents that had been generated in the aftermath of earlier projects. This sounded interesting. With a little help,. I found the documents he had described. Four projects of similar purpose and magnitude had been carried out by the company over the last 12 years or so. At the end of each project, a selection of people who had been directly and significantly involved had been gathered together and asked to brainstorm what had gone well and what had not gone well. The raw brainstormed results were all documented, and some conclusions and summaries had been written.

This seemed a gold mine of data to me. At the next meeting of the planning team, I suggested a formal and structured review of this information as early as possible, in order to identify the most important current and past knowledge and help identify areas requiring attention, as mentioned above. The proposal was well received by the group, with that bit of hesitation reserved for considering something new. Then I realized the importance of that moment. If I had not stumbled across these documents, there would have been no such review. The value of the knowledge represented there would have been lost or would have had to be re-created for the current project. What an amazing irony— "lessons learned" had been built into each project, but they had been planned only at the end, where they could have absolutely no impact!

I do not mean to pat myself much on the back here, since I had never thought of this before myself. I had participated in exercises like those which produced the lessons learned. I had participated in, led, and facilitated countless projects over my career. I had defined steps like "review of best practices" during the early phases of such projects, but the thought of a thorough, structured process (I called it a "pre-learning" exercise) to inventory and highlight the organization's best knowledge hadn't quite occurred to me. More importantly, it simply had never been the norm to include that kind of investigation as part of every major project plan. The operating assumption had always been that the subject matter experts—often those who had contributed to the lessons learned exercises in the first place—would apply their historical knowledge as part of their role in the new project. Even in those circumstances, there was no specifically structured event to cause those people to review the actual "lessons learned" documents. They were just supposed to remember.

This assumption created a critical opportunity gap. While subject matter experts could be reasonably relied upon to execute at least as well as the last time they were called upon, there was no guarantee that they would remember all of their own learning from previous work, and some opportunity for them to improve the quality of their contribution was inevitably lost. (In illustration of this, I would point to the fact that all of the people who participated in the major project I referred to above, when presented with copies of the lessons learned documents, found significant input *of their own* that they had forgotten.) Additionally, since there was no structured review involving other stakeholders in the process, there was less opportunity to identify major systems which worked at some less-than-optimal level. By the time the need for improvement of such systems was recognized, the systems were already in use in the project, making them that much more difficult—and risky—to change.

Do not lose the opportunity, especially at the outset of vital efforts by your organization, to assemble your intellectual resources for a full dress review. Intuitively, it just makes good sense to "mine" your organization for its current knowledge relevant to the purpose and activities of a major project. After all, the organization already "owns" this knowledge. It is there to be had for no more than the time of those who hold it in their heads, and it usually represents thousands to hundreds of thousands of dollars worth of raw data. It may represent millions or even billions of dollars worth of opportunity. Even a marginally successful use of this technique is likely to uncover current knowledge that will ultimately lead to savings of one to two percent of the project budget. In cases where significant opportunities to learn are identified and exploited, this kind of pre-learning activity can identify savings of five percent or more in a project budget.

Here's how to do this:

- Assemble a group of people with a broad spectrum of involvement in previous projects and/or theoretical knowledge in relevant areas. Provide them in advance with copies of any lessons learned-type information. Design a structured group decision process (again, if you want to know how to do this, look at Romig's <u>Breakthrough Teamwork</u>; there is also a discussion of brainstorming technique in Chapter 10) for the group to use in doing the following:
    o Add their own new knowledge and any new thoughts derived from review of the lessons learned to the existing data.
    o Prioritize the input based on their perception of overall impact on the project.
    o Establish connections between the data and the processes or systems within the organization which they affect and which they come from. Use this process to "cluster" bits of the raw data where they all relate to one system.
    o Give input on estimated potential cost impact of the areas identified for attention.
    o Brainstorm solutions for high-priority opportunities.
    o Highlight areas which seem to be chronic issues for special attention by management early in the process.
- Use the information generated by this review wisely. It is invaluable.

- ***Learn how to state a proper learning objective. Review project plans for required behavior changes. Define them as learning objectives, and design appropriate learning for each such***

> *change. Focus at least as much on decision making as activity; correct execution depends first on correct decisions.*

A long time ago, I was taught how to state a learning objective. A learning objective, it turns out, has some specific and critical characteristics. Most interestingly, it does not focus on learning at all; it focuses on behavior. A well-stated learning objective states how a learner's behavior will specifically change (or at least be enabled to change) as a result of a particular instructional event. It also includes a description of the level of proficiency or measure of performance to be expected as a result of that event. This sounds pretty easy. In practice, it is often difficult to do well, especially if the learning at hand has theoretical components. Consider the following:

Upon completion of the training the participant will understand how to use process history data in establishing statistical process control limits for a process.

It may sound like a learning objective, but it's not—at least not a very good one. Although the sentence makes it sound as though learning is happening, there is in fact no description of changed *behavior*. Without changed behavior—application, as we have referred to it in this book— no real learning takes place. A good way of knowing whether behavior is affected is by asking yourself if you could see it. You can't see and certainly can't measure "understanding," which is what the above objective claims will be provided. An improvement might look like this:

Upon completion of this training, the participant will be able to access and download historical data for a desired process, analyze that data by selecting and using established statistical methods, and recommend appropriate statistical process limits and charting methods.

As you see, there are three specific, observable behaviors defined in this statement: accessing and downloading data, analyzing data, and recommending limits and charts. In order for it to be a "proper" learning objective, there really ought to be a bit more attention given to the expected level of proficiency. That is not, however, what I want you to learn right now. I want you to focus on the change of behavior, and to remember that changed behavior and learning are inextricably linked. Note also, that this objective highlights key decisions that will have to be made: selecting appropriate analysis tools and making recommendations for improvement. This is a <u>crucial and often overlooked</u> part of a learning objective. Without a focus on this part of the learning, we risk having the learner approach new tasks knowing how—but not <u>why</u>—to do them. Additionally, without this focus, the new practitioner will face a higher likelihood of confusion (and thus delay) if any circumstances are encountered that were not specifically addressed in the training—and such circumstances will inevitably be encountered.

Learning to state learning objectives makes you more sensitive to changes in behavior. Use that sensitivity to look at project plans and identify where behavior changes—and therefore learning—will be required. Use all of the skills we have discussed to address that learning.

- Do this at the same time as you review projects for information hand-offs, as described above. Establish actions in the plan to address the identified learning needs in the most appropriate and effective way.

- **Develop structured processes to learn from experience—especially bad experience.**

I have previously advised you to become an expert at identifying soft spots. You might recall that I acknowledged this might prove a threat to your popularity. If reputation or relationships have suffered from your taking that advice, I apologize—and I offer this possible way to gain some small redemption. If you are the person who can bring to your organization—be that a company, a family, a government agency, etc.—a process that will allow the members to review experience (*especially* bad experience) for learning without emotional injury, you can be a hero.

Learning from good experience is pretty easy, though even that can require a surprising amount of attention. We have already discussed one structured way to learn from experience: the pre-learning exercise described above. Mostly, however, that assumed a review of earlier projects with mostly good, or at worst benign, results. It is generally pretty easy to get people to participate whole-heartedly in a review of such results.

The truth is that learning from bad experience can also be pretty easy; it is sharing that learning which makes for issues. I have seen few organizations able to do this effectively and consistently. When I have discovered organizations that did this well, they have been relatively small groups within larger organizations, islands of excellence. Intel is reputed to have a culture which manages this well, if a little confrontationally; the process is referred to there as a *post mortem*.

The issue of course is blame, with humiliation close in the running. Remember the Improvement Engine and the source of the data being reviewed; it is the application data, the data which reflect people's *actual performance*. We have already discussed the natural sensitivities to be expected in treating with this data. It is sometimes difficult, especially in the wake of major catastrophe, to distinguish between those who are involved in a problem and what is actually responsible for the problem. Blame may be attached as a result of simple proximity—the "you were the last one with it" syndrome. However it happens, if the investigation of painful events is perceived to produce victims more than learning, the process will founder or simply become a recognized Inquisition, against which one can only defend oneself, and where truth may not be the arbiter of justice.

Two things are required to learn consistently and successfully from bad experience:

1) You must use a structured process that ensures unbiased assembling of data, presentation of data, analysis of information,

and establishing of conclusions. Use structure to diminish emotion.

2) Establish a tradition. Structure alone won't convince people to participate in this to the fullest until they have seen the process at work and concluded that it is safe. Only time and repetition will allow you to accomplish this.

I will return to this topic again when the Engine is completed and again in discussion of leadership issues. In the meantime, here are some things you can do to start working on this:

- Get in touch with your own pain. Examine your greatest personal failures. Identify what you really learned and how you have changed your behavior since to accommodate that learning. If you are like most folks, there should be a little discomfort in this process. Remember that and the fact that any process used by a group to do this must involve some public exposure of that same discomfort.

- Design a process that is repeatable and unbiased for groups to use in examining and learning from a painful past event. For guidance in defining effective group processes, I again recommend Romig's <u>Breakthrough Teamwork</u>. Other facilitator guides exist that may provide you with ideas. If you have a Human Resources or especially an Organizational Development group as a resource, ask for their input.

- Define ground rules for maintaining mutual self-respect in the process. You will need to be obsessively consistent in following these rules, so be prepared to enforce them.

- Don't forget to learn from the good experiences, either. Be as relentless at discovering what you do well as you are at rooting out your deficiencies. Make sure those discoveries are shared throughout your organization

- *Examine relationships with suppliers and customers—and even across groups within your own organization—for possible learning opportunities—especially free ones!*

I do not mean to recommend industrial espionage here. I simply mean that you should look at what your suppliers and customers do well and learn as much as possible from that. It is not OK to copy technology; that's called stealing. It seems to be generally agreed, however, that it's OK to "steal" behavior through observation; that is called imitating. Since you enjoy a (hopefully) mutually profitable relationship, they may be more willing than others to give you some insight into their methods as long as trade secrets are not involved. In many cases, such cooperation may cost you nothing more than the time to learn, as they are likely to be motivated to help assure your continuing presence as an economic "partner." This is especially likely if you have some best practices of your own to offer for their improvement. Obviously, this is possible within your organization as well. There are undoubtedly groups who do things better than others; find out what they are and set the learning process in motion!

The biggest problem with doing this is probably getting past N.I.H.: "Not Invented Here." For anybody unfamiliar with this syndrome, it refers to the resistance of a person or group to outside ideas—the idea that "we can fix our problems without help from outsiders, thank you." I like confidence. I enjoy seeing people who are proud of their capabilities. I am saddened, however, when I see that pride turn to ego-based defensiveness. I consider it especially disappointing when it is visible within organizations supposedly pursuing a common interest. Like many aspects of resistance to change in general, it seems to be almost a bit of human nature. That's no excuse. After all, most real success requires the subordination of some aspect of "human nature." We become great by overcoming our weaknesses, not by pandering to them.

I suggest two specific actions to move you ahead in this area:

- Know your strengths. Actively seek out the activities and processes that work best and get the most favorable comments from external and internal sources.
- Make a point of establishing learning relationships between your organization and others. If this happens at the organizational level, internal groups will be more likely to resist N.I.H. themselves.

Reflection:

- Since I have spent the whole chapter telling you things to do, there is only one reflection:

    - Review this chapter and select a few (2 for the hesitant, 5 for the aggressive) of these points to turn into personal learning assignments. (As I have already mentioned, if you only do *one* thing from this chapter, at least start paying close attention to the preparation for and follow-up after assigned training.) Set a learning plan for yourself, and start applying those techniques. Add more when you are ready.

- Oh, there is one other reflection: Learners are examples whether they try to be or not. If you start changing your behavior as this chapter suggests, other people will notice. Do not be dismissive of the impact this may have, especially if you are perceived as a leader in your organization.

Chapter 6

Finishing the Improvement Engine

"The people I distrust most are those who want to improve our lives but have only one course of action."
Frank Herbert

Up to this point, we have really been dealing with concepts and tools that have been discussed and understood by others, albeit perhaps not in relation to such a nice, compact, explanatory model as the Improvement Engine—and not relative to a set of foundational equations like the Physics of Success. Many of the behaviors in the previous chapter, especially those having to do with the preparation for and immediate application of new learning and customizing learning processes to the need, are also part of a set of practices long known to effectively support performance improvement. Some of the behaviors in that last chapter are, however, (as far as I know) inventions or at least emphases of my own (e.g., "pre-learning," the idea of regarding all communication as potential learning, and understanding learning as a critical part of cycle time).

Now, however, I hope to bring something distinctly new to our discussion. In this chapter, I will show you how I finished building the Engine. It's just a matter of adding four parts, but when we examine the finished Engine, I think you will find that things have changed dramatically. Within these four remarkably similar Engine parts are the explanation for <u>why</u> proven improvement techniques and strategies build strong, successful organizations and how leaders can influence the pace of learning, even accelerating the benefits from using currently successful tools and processes.

By the way, as I get into this chapter, I will start referring to the processes and people on the left hand side of the diagram as Invention and Inventors (with anachronistic capitals). On the right hand side of the diagram, I will refer to Application and Appliers. It should help ease our conversation.

Final Assembly

Let's start by taking another look at the Engine as we left it at the end of Chapter 4:

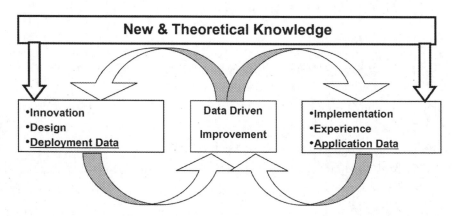

After I got this far, I thought about the Engine in this state for several months, trying to find what was missing. Oh, there was something missing, all right; I knew that. All this model did so far was confirm the already (to me, at least) inescapable logic of advocating continuous process improvement. Admittedly, it was sound, accurate, and compact. I was sure it had value, since it explained so much that I had seen to be effective—and ineffective—in organizational behavior. At last, after months of staring at that model and using it to analyze various situations past and present, I found my attention focused on the box in the middle. Why had that box made so much difference? What had really changed to allow the objectivity of data to become the arbiter of meeting behavior and personal interactions (for, certainly, the people of the organizations around me treated each other differently—better—both in public and in private since we started using these techniques)? I had originally thought that it was a consequence of the box itself—that data and information exchange were both the root causes and root enablers of better learning and, therefore, according to the Physics, the causes and enablers of success. The more I thought about it, though, the more I realized that the most important changes, the ones that really made a difference in how well various groups used data-based decision-making, had been not in the processes, but in the people themselves. For instance, take this simple observation: people in these groups were now willing to talk about and listen to things that had been previously withheld or ignored. Nothing in the diagram showed that. In fact, as I realized at last and with some mild shock, nothing in the diagram reflected people at all.

That was the breakthrough that allowed me to define the last four parts of the Engine. In the context of our continuing comparison to automobile technology, I think these four parts correspond closely to the cooling, carburetion, and filtration systems. Their position and function in the Engine occurred to me as I tried to define the human aspect of the changes I had seen while simultaneously focusing on the idea that all communication (transfer of data) is potential learning. One thing that occurred to me in my various analyses of past and present situations was that failure, when it occurred, seemed most often to have its root cause not within any of the boxes, but at their interfaces. (One common exception to that conclusion, by the way, was poor planning, which mostly belongs on the left side—the "Invention" side—of the Engine. "Poor planning" includes promising more than you can deliver—a fault whose consequences often seem to land with the executing group.) The problems seemed to be traceable to failures in understanding, valuing, learning from, and/or acting appropriately on data received from others in the organization. Failures which at first appeared to be in execution—the "Application" side of the Engine—were often, upon deeper inquiry, caused by a failure of the executing group to understand (or adequately value!) the instructions or planning and therefore had their root cause at the communication interfaces, not actually within the right-hand box.

When it comes to trust, outputs are hard to distinguish from the people who provide them, so actual execution failures often have an effect on interpersonal trust, and vice versa.

The word that best described what made the difference in exchange of information was "trust." As I thought about that word, I realized it acted in concert with another kind of trust: the word for that was "respect." Because of agreement on the simple idea that data, not personalities or authority, would drive decision making, people felt they could <u>trust</u> others with <u>all</u> of the data on the issues they were facing, without concern that being so forthcoming might only clarify where to assign blame. People receiving data now demonstrated, in both their behaviors and attitudes, a new <u>respect</u> for the information and learning they might get from others. This was partly due to trust as well; they had faith that nothing was being kept from them, that data were not massaged to make problems (and thus opportunities) invisible.

Let's put "trust" in the Engine diagram wherever data leaves a group and put "respect" wherever data enters a group. If we do that, the Engine looks like this:

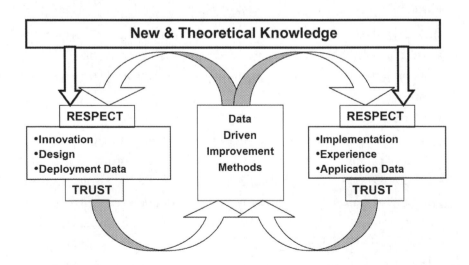

(Note that I have also moved the arrows from "New and Theoretical Knowledge" so that they also intersect the "RESPECT" boxes.)

Let me help you get a vision of your own Engine at work as affected by these new parts. Imagine that you are approached by a person (the Inventor of this cycle) who gives you (the intended Applier) information and asks you to take specific action based on that information. One problem—you either don't trust the information or you don't trust the person. Do you act slowly or quickly? Why? Are other aspects of your work affected, such as quality? What does this imply?

If you are really pushing yourself to learn here, DO NOT continue reading. STOP and look at what these changes to the Engine do to the system. Draw your own conclusions before you go on to read my explanation. It's OK. It's worth it. I can wait. If I have had my way with my publisher, there is either a removable or easy-to-copy version of the Improvement Engine in this book. Post a copy of the Engine where it will be visible when you are thinking deep thoughts, and use it to analyze your own events (remember, the ones I asked you to write down at the beginning of the book?).

Here are some questions to consider in this exercise. When you originally experienced these events:

- What information (or misinformation) prompted Inventors to take action? Where did it come from?
- What made the Inventors trust/respect the source (or not)?
- Was the plan/design developed in communication with the Appliers?
- What level of faith did the Inventors have in the ability of the Appliers to understand and execute?
- In meetings among themselves, did Appliers praise or belittle the efforts of the Inventors? To what degree and to what effect? Ask the same questions with regard to Inventors.
- How forthcoming were the Appliers in providing information about their performance, especially the sub-optimal kind?
- Did Appliers do a good job of highlighting the best areas for Inventors to work on for improvement?

- Were Application data subjected to rigorous, objective analysis to produce conclusions that all parties could support (consensus)?
- How much attention did Inventors pay to Applier feedback? How did future plans/designs/actions of the Inventors reflect that?
- What level of respect was evident between leaders of Inventing and Applying organizations?

. . . and, most important of all:

- **How did trust and respect, both of information and those providing it, affect the speed, quality, or volume of execution, learning, and improvement?**

By the way, shortly after I finished the Engine, somebody asked me if there weren't some way to make it just a bit simpler. The simplified diagram that resulted I offer here as well. It streamlines the functions of the boxes and makes the whole thing an easily memorable set of parts. Note that it has one final modification: the center box has been renamed "Teach." It occurred to me that all the methods we had learned to make our "communication" better and improve our decision making abilities had been about using data and structure to "teach" people about problems, options, priorities, etc., so they could make decisions quickly and act in confidence. (Note that "data" is the filter coming into the "Teach" box; data is the entrance requirement; it is your primary tool for establishing trust in your data itself, in your conclusions, and in your recommendations.)

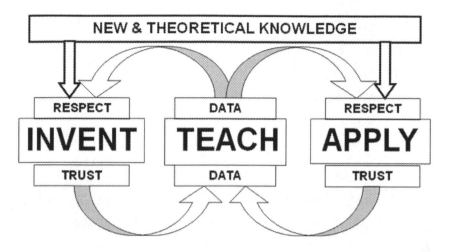

Go think a while. I'll be right here when you get back.

===

Welcome back! What did you see?

Is it intuitively true to you that differing degrees of trust would affect the quality and quantity of information you would willingly provide to others? Is it also equally intuitively true that your trust of information received from others, i.e., the value that you place upon it and thus the respect that you give it, is affected by your respect for and trust of the source? Does your analysis of events in the context of the completed Engine lead you to the conclusion that I came to above, that failure's root cause, though initially supposed to lie with a particular group or function, is often found at the interfaces rather than in the boxes themselves?

I hope that the answers to those three questions were all "yes." If not, it seems likely to me that any "no" answer would probably be to the third question; the first two, I feel, are pretty much rhetorical and, when answered affirmatively, simply reflect natural human behavior. If you think the first question is a "no," and if you are not yet convinced that the interfaces are responsible for more trouble than is readily apparent,

I suggest we agree to disagree at the moment and see if you still feel the same way on this issue at the end of the book.

As I said in the first chapter, almost all meaningful improvement requires changing people as well as processes, products, and services. The Engine should give you a better picture of how information, learning, and trust affect the speed and quality of human change. Fail to get the people part right, and even the best improvement attempts can easily fail.

I would like to introduce a final personal note here which has, I believe, important implications. When I completed this diagram, I came to a new understanding of my career. I always had a passion for Quality, as an organization or function, which I could not put into words. I admit to having been a bit of a zealot about it—and probably still am. As I looked at this diagram, however, I realized that Quality had always been about building trust. Internally, that trust was built with process, system, and incoming material controls; externally, Quality was tasked to provide data to customers that would specifically affect their trust of our product. I had always been a campaigner for trust, but I had never attached that particular word to my passion, nor had I realized the pervasive effect of trust in every aspect of organizational performance. Trust, like quality, cannot be an event or a program; it must be institutional, an enduring system of relationships. Quality has a lot to do with understanding how predictable processes and products are, and predictability is a close relative of trust. Thus our natural tendency to fear and resist change, because of the unpredictability of outcomes. (Racism can be somewhat explained, though certainly not excused, on this basis. Cultural differences ultimately can result in behaviors not predictable by other cultures. Suspicion and/or ridicule are the all-too-frequent reactions.)

Let's go on to talk about the conclusions I have to offer based on the Improvement Engine in its completed state.

A First Run Through

Let's start by just following the path of information through one loop of the cycle, with a brief examination of fundamental issues involved at each step—sort of like hand-cranking the Engine just to turn it over once.

Step 1: Inventors receive data and start to innovate.

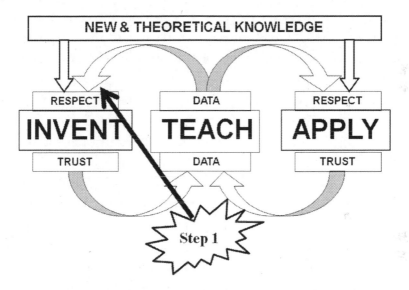

Everything starts in the left-hand corner with an infusion of information, either from internal (Application data or input from a Data Driven Improvement Strategy—I'll have a good deal more to say about this exchange when we come across it again at the end of the cycle) or external (New & Theoretical) sources. The reaction to that information is some Innovation, beginning the process of Invention. Any knowledge or information entering the Invention function is first screened, or filtered, by the respect of the receiving group for that information and its source. Remember that respect does not always mean admiration; our own bad experiences and those of others are often useful learning tools, even though we do not typically seek adversity and failure as teaching sources. It is probably useful to bear in mind Chris Argyris's Ladder of Inference when thinking about how this filter acts. (There will be a more detailed discussion of the Ladder of Influence in the next chapter.) At the lowest level of the Ladder is our ability to observe. From what we (1) observe, we (2) select certain data and (3) attach meaning and a level of importance to that data. Based on our perception of the importance of the selected data, we (4) make assumptions, from which we generalize to (5) establish beliefs. Finally, from a basis of beliefs, we (6) make decisions and (7) take action. This "Respect" filter is acting directly on steps 2 and 3 of the Ladder. Consider what is at stake here. First (step 1 on the Ladder), we must hope that our Inventing groups are in touch with the right information sources so that they will even have an opportunity to see all, or at least most, of the data that might be important to their success. Studies have shown, however, that even scientists hardened to research procedures and the objective observation of phenomena may simply, completely, and literally fail to even observe data that suggest conclusions too far removed from what they expect. Hoping that nothing critical is screened out, we must now face the fact that any information seen must be selected (step 2); it must be chosen as interesting enough for further examination. What are the distinguishers for interesting versus uninteresting data? One, I can assure you, is probably the first and the biggest: do you or do you not believe the data? We have entered the world of trust. Is your belief in the data affected by your faith in its source? Of course it is! Is your faith in any source affected by your respect of that source? Again, of course it is. Trust and its handmaiden, respect, are critically engaged in determining what your Inventing groups even listen to. Finally, any incoming information must pass one more hurdle (step 3 on the Ladder) before it can have any significant effect; it must be perceived as important. Once again, trust and respect of the information and its source will play a huge part in what is screened out and what is used to drive the process of Invention.

Step 2: The Inventors innovate and release data/design.

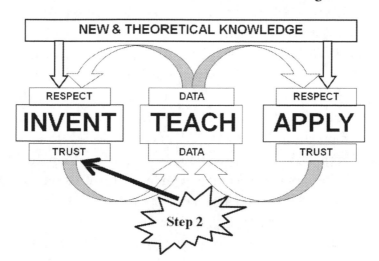

Having followed their own Ladder of Inference to its final rung, the Inventing group will take action on the beliefs they have formed from the data they used. They will innovate, create a design, and pass that design on to the world of Application. Consider what this means. In the world of industry, such efforts are usually major. There is a tremendous investment of time, energy, creativity, and determination required to get a new product or strategy into actual production or use. These investments are organizational, but they are personal as well. Each person involved will have a certain sense of ownership in the group's output. Now, however, the Inventors will be asked to share, if not give up, that ownership to Appliers. In many ways, they will be like Dwight Eisenhower in the minutes after the decision to go ahead with the D-Day invasion. Up to that moment, he had been the most powerful man on two continents. At the moment of that decision, however, all his ability to affect the final outcome vanished and was delegated on to thousands of subordinate leaders, each with a particular goal and one overriding mission: the invasion of Europe. Eisenhower undoubtedly trusted them with his plan, despite the horrible risks involved. Do the Inventing functions in your organization have that same confidence in the Application functions? That trust would be generated by a history of successful executions to commitments, both at the organizational and the personal levels. What would be the consequences of lack of trust on the part of an Inventing group in such a situation? We might anticipate a few options. First, if they do not particularly trust the people or the group with whom they are interacting, we can be assured that communication will be minimal, designed only to fill requirements. Second, we might have some concern that quality of the plan/design might suffer because lack of confidence has fostered a lack of enthusiasm, concern, or attention, leading to a sub-optimal result. Third, we could see the generation of an inter-organizational conflict if Inventors, unwilling to abandon control of their ideas to Appliers whom they do not trust, attempt to influence or control functions beyond their organizational boundaries. I don't know about you, but I, at least, have seen all these things. None of them improved anything except the list of bad examples for future learning.

Step 2a: Data is passed on using (hopefully) best data driven improvement techniques to teach people the new idea.

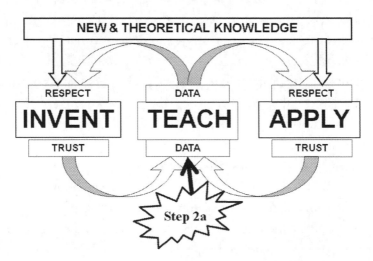

It may seem a bit confusing at this point to talk about improvement. After all, nothing has yet been done, and how can something which has not yet been done be improved? The answer to this seeming contradiction is reflected in a whole field of quality probably best summed up as Design for Manufacturability (DFM). This concept has been "marketed" under various names and acronyms (see Chapter 7), but the underlying point is this: if an organization has taken on the mantle of Continuous Improvers, the plan/design will move through the Data Driven Improvement Strategies box on its way to Application. In here, hopefully, data about expectations and capabilities can be compared, analyzed, and turned into collaborative decisions about how best to deploy the work of the Inventors. Once again, trust can be enhanced by these procedures. (I might be tempted to rename this area of continuous improvement "DFT": Design For Trust.) The old system of simply throwing the design "over the wall" to the Appliers damages trust on both sides of the wall. In such a case, neither Inventors nor Appliers have any assurance that the design is even practicable. The result is a ripe opportunity for failure and blame. The job here is to use data to validate and teach your point.

Step 3: Appliers receive data.

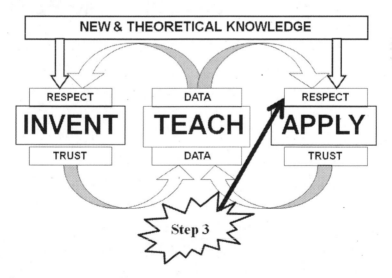

Despite the complications and pitfalls, designs and plans do make their way to Application groups. Here, in the "RESPECT" box on the "APPLY" side of the diagram, the boundaries of, screens to, and filters for information are pretty much the same as with Inventing organizations, and they work in generally the same manner. There is one factor that makes for quite a difference in receiving information, however; the Application group is generally required to respond to pretty much all of the expectations defined by the Inventing group. There is less allowance, if any, on their part to select what information they will value. If a lack of trust/respect exists between the groups, the Application group may perceive themselves to be at the mercy of the Invention group—expected to make real the Inventors' ideas despite any lack of quality or capability inherent in the plan/design itself.

Step 4: Appliers execute and release data.

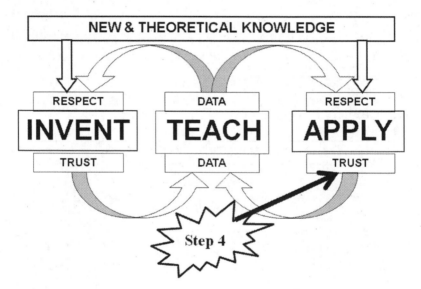

Once the Application group starts making or doing something, it will start to generate a history of experience. Raw data will be generated. Performance statistics will be analyzed. Summaries will be written. This information may be tedious to assemble and may not seem, especially to those assembling it, to add much value, so motivation may be somewhat feeble. People will be interested in that information, however, and there will often be incredible value hidden in its nooks and crannies. Its owners, however, will pass any information they release through their own filter of trust for the receivers. If the organization routinely imposes severe consequences for reporting unfavorable data and Appliers do not trust that the data will be used for its best and most objective effects, they will do their best to present all information in only the most positive light. Usually this involves some "massaging" of the data—not outright deception, but a bit of sleight-of-hand that distracts from any negative information. Of course, removing or diverting attention from the signals in the data that might attract unwelcome scrutiny typically castrates the data; any real learning and improvement opportunities end up being obscured or ignored. When you are given only a half-truth, there is seldom a reliable way to determine which half you have in hand.

As we have already discussed, the data proceeding from Application reflects the actual ability of people to perform and may be very sensitive to its owners. I have seen organizations where Application groups could bring their problems—even outright failures!—to the table without fear, in the certain knowledge that improvement, not blame, was the object of the organization. I have also seen the reverse. I remember one day, early in my career, walking into a restroom at work to find a production manager vomiting in the sink. I naturally asked if he was OK. He told me that he was on his way to the monthly Operations Review for his group, and that the results he would be showing were not up to expectations. I knew the director for that group, and the manager and I both knew that no explanation was necessary for the connection between the vomiting and the upcoming meeting. The director had a reputation for bullying and humiliating, in public, presenters who had anything but glowing results. Incidentally, neither that director nor his organization was particularly successful in the long run. Now, let's get back to tracing information through the Engine . . .

Particularly in the case of data from Application, there may be an effect on the data provided based on the respect given that information in the receiving Invention group—or even the amount of trust established in the hand-offs of information from the Inventing group in previous development cycles. This seems to sometimes be an observable self-fulfilling prophecy in a predictable cycle: 1) It starts with a history—at least as perceived by the Appliers—of the Inventors abusing their organizational mandate to create things for the Appliers to do. Inventors are perceived as ignorant of, indifferent to, or (worst) arrogant regarding the constraints and realities of the Appliers' world. 2) The Invention group displays little regard for opinions or conclusions of the Appliers, and sometimes little regard for the hard data as well. 3) The Appliers, who perceive that expectations for their input are low, meet those expectations. This phenomenon seems unique to the exchange of data from Appliers to Inventors, which is why I didn't bring up this same general concern when I talked about the exchange from Inventors to Appliers. As I have also mentioned, this exchange is almost always supported by organizational mandate—and rightly so, since no organization can survive which does not turn its ideas to actions. The former exchange, however, from Appliers to Inventors, is not always so mandated. If the organization is not determined to learn from its experience (that is, if leaders from both sides of the Engine do not show mutual regard for each other, their organizations, and the data they exchange), it may become easiest for the organization to dismiss the input of Appliers as just a drone of constant problem identification.

Step 4a: Data is passed on using (hopefully) best data driven improvement techniques to drive learning and subsequent new ideas.

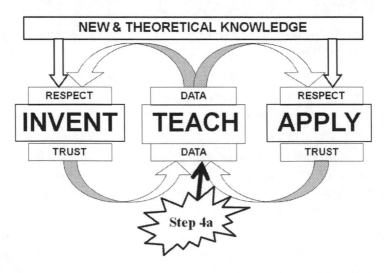

The logic from Step 2a, plus a host of other reasons that have now become apparent, would only raise our hopes that such systems are in place. Again, the purpose here is to use data to teach—in this case, to teach others about what has actually happened.

Step 5 (or part of Step 1 again, depending on how you look at it): Application data comes to the Inventors.

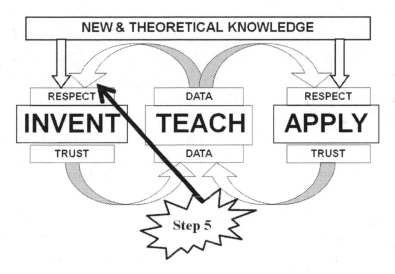

Now let's look at the last step in the cycle of the Engine: the transfer of data into the Invention group(s) from the Appliers. Just because of the discussion above, don't think I'm letting the Appliers off the hook for their issues with releasing information. Organizational mandate may give the Inventors a bit of an unfair advantage, but who said the world was fair? No matter what the excuse/reason, the Appliers must accept that a burden lies with them for hampering the organization's success if the Inventors do not have the most complete and best analyzed picture of Application data possible. It is obvious that they will learn less, and therefore improve less, without it. Data-driven improvement skills have a strong hand in improving the interface between Appliers and Inventors. Key among those skills are the gathering, analysis, and presentation of data. In the past, the Appliers I was watching when I developed this model had only elementary skills in this area, and they could often neither identify the existence nor argue the meaning of statistically important events. As a result, they were prone to simply pronouncing current results "unacceptable" (one of my *favorite* business words) and demanding improvement. Quite frankly, they deserved their lack of credibility as a source of information for improvement, since they did not have the skills to <u>make</u> themselves credible. When they did learn those skills, however, they gained the attention, and very quickly the respect, of the Inventors. The Inventors, now with a reasonable level of trust that the problems/opportunities identified to them by the Appliers were real and probably the most critical, responded and fixed or improved, as appropriate. The Appliers, seeing the evidence of response to their issues, got excited and identified even more. Everyone worked together to find and implement solutions and improvements. The cycle continued, more processes improved, relationships improved (success is a great morale builder), the Engine turned faster . . . it was just glorious, I tell you.

Remember this: Well, that was a first run. Of course, as with mechanical engines, turning it once over slowly doesn't tell you a lot about what happens when the thing really gets rolling. However, there are three main things I would like to make sure you take from this demonstration cycle into a deeper analysis of what happens as the Engine itself moves out of the womb of Invention and into the world of Application. Those two main points are:

- **Success has four human hurdles**. There are four separate and distinct points where every vision, decision, process, action, plan, design, goal, intent, or hope can fail based on the respect or trust allowed to the flow of knowledge and learning. (When I first wrote this, I asked myself why I had focused on the possibility for failure in that last sentence, instead of success. It would have been a bit more like my optimistic self to have talked about how those trust and respect boxes can lead to success. After thinking a bit, I decided that, first of all, I have just seen too many pointless and easy-to-avoid failures at these points; avoiding them has become a primary concern of mine and a factor in planning and decision-making from the start of all projects. Second, despite my general disregard for fear as a motivator, I do want you to have a healthy fear of what can happen when things go wrong inside those boxes.)

- **Trust and truth are strongly linked.** In an organization where trust is high, one can act with confidence on the data provided by colleagues, since it will most likely be the truth or at least the communicator's best understanding of the truth. Low trust will lead to (justified) suspicion and second-guessing (since information will typically be released in a manner designed to mask any "unfortunate" results). Worse yet, your organization might end up acting in a world of genuine disinformation, either tilting at ethereal windmills (e.g., doing things customers don't care about), or basking in an emperor's clothes (e.g., assuming all is well as customer confidence, in fact, erodes).

- **You must gain control over an idea to make it productive, and controls and processes to do this help build trust, but you can go too far.** Over-rigid control systems, originally designed to minimize variation or reduce risk but evolved into an oppressive burden, are more resistant to change and thus resist improvement as well. Additionally, if there is simply too much cumbersome procedure around approving change, people with good ideas will give up on getting them implemented, seeing the benefit as not worth the effort and frustration.

Before we run this Engine, we should understand the symptoms and some of the underlying causes of poor Engine performance. This will help us know what to look for in managing it. Here is a quick list of conditions that may be indicators of high or low levels of trust in an organization, process, product, or service:

LOW TRUST INDICATORS .... HIGH TRUST INDICATORS

High Risk .... Low Risk

Input(s)/Outputs Unreliable ....Input(s)/Outputs Reliable

Process Not Capable .... Process Capable

Many/High Level Signatures ....No Signatures

Multiple, Rigorous Controls .... No Controls

Win/Lose Expectation .... Win/Win Expectation

Unilateral Concerns ....Mutual Concerns

Communication on Need.................... Continuous Communication

Purpose/Goal Unclear .... Purpose/Goal Clear

Method Unknown/Doubtful ....Clear, Proven Method

As you look at these indicators, you should also be able to see that improving performance is not simply a matter of maximizing trust. There are decisions that *should* require more than one person's approval to implement. Some processes *should* have high levels of control. Sometimes you really *are* in a win-lose situation, or you must work with people who care only about their own needs and agendas. Best performance will come from balancing these to optimal—not simply maximized—levels.

Now that we know what to watch out for, let's go ahead and fire this Engine up, shall we?

Idling

There is no "firing up" to be done, really. You undoubtedly noticed that it was already running as soon as you put it together and put people in it. Note as well that the Engine idles at high speed—very high speed. As I pointed out in Chapter 4, this Engine is always running. It runs in individuals, it runs in small groups, and it runs in the most megalithic organizations, always on, always processing at a practically breakneck pace. If there is no specifically directed input of information, the Engine will suck in data at random, and people will interpret and find meaning, make decisions, create plans and designs, and take action. In fact, if an Engine can be deprived entirely of external fuel it will still, through the wonder of imagination, get fuel by generating its own information. Even if there is no expected result, the Engine will run anyway, and people will produce things they find meaningful. This, basically, is why we have art. Humans seem driven to turn idea into action, so that action may produce imagined and desired results. As Abraham Maslow pointed out, there is a certain hierarchy to our needs (for a brief explanation of Maslow's hierarchy, see "References and Notes" in this book); most of us have to have sufficient food, water, and shelter before we can turn our attention to, for instance, building model ships or writing sonnets. (It must be admitted, though, that the tradition of the suffering artist shows how the passion of some ideas, or the obsessions of their owners, can invert even these hierarchies.) Every hobby store, sporting goods store, and a good chunk of every hardware store is a manifestation of the idling Engine.

Actually, the concept of idling is a little hard to even apply here, since the Engine begins to generate energy and direction on its own if left unguided and uncontrolled. In our continuing automotive analogy, think of the consequences of driving a car that you can't turn off. (Just be thankful that the fuel—knowledge—is available for free everywhere, especially since these Engines guzzle it like cold root beer on the Fourth of July. It can also be re-used, and the same bit of knowledge may be used to fuel many separate Engines, with each Engine still able to get the full benefit. Gasoline, in this light, is a poor, smelly, and dangerous fuel by comparison.) This car has another problem, by the way; if you park it and leave it to its own devices long enough, it will eventually get ideas and wander off on its own. Perhaps most perplexing in terms of our continuing automotive analogy, consider that the performance of the Engine has a dramatic effect on your vehicle's handling, i.e., its ability to go where you steer it. This is true to the point that, under certain conditions, you may sometimes not be assured of keeping to the road or, perhaps, of even getting to your desired destination, but ending up somewhere else altogether. Imagine getting dirt in your air filter and, consequently, not being able to turn left—unimaginable in a car but quite possible in the Engine-driven organization. When you consider handling, you have to consider the size of the vehicle, and this brings us to another problem in our analogy: scale. There are a lot of one—and two-person vehicles, some vans and stations wagons, buses and RV's for the big groups; these do well to compare to organizations of similar size. There are, however, much, much bigger organizations. Our largest wheeled vehicles, trains, carry a few hundred people at a time, so even they are a bit inadequate in representing truly large organizations. (In terms of handling, though, it should be noted that a vehicle that size cannot be steered except by changing it to different tracks.) In order to get the right picture of a major organization at large in the fields of commerce, I think you must imagine vehicles the size of aircraft carriers, functioning on land. Steering something that big is obviously going to be no small feat on its own, but add in an unruly Engine that routinely deteriorates your steering capability, and you have got a challenge indeed. The consequences of making steering mistakes with something that big are pretty serious as well; in your mind's eye, picture that carrier taking a right too tightly and taking out seven homes (lay-offs), a gas station (failure of captive supplier partner), a Dairy Queen (failure of businesses riding the coattails of your success), and a community center (impact of all the preceding on civic prosperity). It's not what anybody wants.

In the real world, no organization is created without an idea toward its purpose. Thus, if you have taken the steps necessary to gather your own wits as to a purpose, and especially if you have gathered the wits of a few others, then you have already gotten beyond the idling stage. Your Engine took off—with your vehicle—the moment you created the organization, perhaps even the moment you had the idea to create it. At any rate, there's not a lot of point in talking further about the idling

Engine, since you are not likely to be dealing with one, and your's is undoubtedly on its way somewhere as we speak. Go ahead, run and catch up. Just keep in mind that these Engines never turn off, they are voracious in their appetite for knowledge, and they are independent sometimes to the point of orneriness. Your immediate challenge will be to try to balance, and eventually optimize, the following basic parameters of the Engine's operation:

- Alignment of purpose (How easily and accurately does it steer? This is "handling"; we were just talking about this above.)
- Volume of relevant incoming knowledge. (This would be the equivalent of fuel quantity and quality.)
- Speed of transformation: knowledge to action. (This equates to fuel efficiency—how much value you squeeze out of information—as well as to how fast the Engine "turns" and produces results, or its "RPM".)

Are you ready to try it on the road?

General Performance Guidelines

Once again I find I have ended a section with a slightly misleading question. Unless you are anti-social beyond imagination, you are the member of some organization (most of us have several: family, colleagues, friends, etc.—some of those organizations are just the same people aligned in different groups for different purposes), and that means you are on the road already and have been there a while. Most of the people reading this book will, I think, be parts of fairly formal organizations. Many may be in leadership positions and thus rightly feel a responsibility for deciding (or at least influencing) direction and speed of the organization.

Properly speaking, then, the first challenges you may face in driving your Engine-powered organization may not be exactly intuitive. For instance, you may first have to catch it, if it has, in fact, wandered off without you. Furthermore, if your Engine has been running for rather a while on matters of its own choosing, you may find that (to borrow a metaphor from an even older mode of transportation) it has gotten its bit between its teeth and is reluctant to relinquish control. If the organization is large, these control issues escalate. As the number of minds within the organization grows, the energy of the system increases at a greater-than-linear rate. That energy will not be subdued, though it may be encouraged, and if not well channeled it will find its outlet anyway, sapping your organization of opportunities as it focuses on other learning—learning which, by virtue of necessity or creative intent, captures members' interests. The more such undirected outlets there are, the more they will affect the ability of the organization to respond to directional commands.

Metaphorically speaking, such conditions seem absurd. How can one reasonably hope to pilot such a juggernaut? Not only is it huge, it has a mind of its own. Even on a good day it is hard to steer, and it seems to accelerate and brake for reasons only distantly related to your wishes. You might reasonably protest, if such a vehicle were offered to you, that you do not want this Engine; you want another, less unruly model. I must regretfully inform you that: 1) this is the only Engine model available; 2) they come with all organizations, at no extra charge; and 3) they cannot actually be removed from organizations without removing all the people—which pretty much makes it not an organization any more, much less a successful one. The organization and the Engine are inseparable, so your best bet is just to learn how your's runs best *(They all need just a bit different tuning, did I mention that?)* and try to get it to guide itself as much as possible.

Remember that steering, and thus direction, are at the mercy of the Engine. If there were a corollary in the mechanical world, it might be in the area of tracked vehicles such as bulldozers and tanks. Steering tracked vehicles requires balancing the speed of one track against the other. To go straight, both tracks must run at the same speed. Increase the speed of the right track only, and you will turn left, and vice versa. This is in itself a good deal more complicated than typical motor vehicle steering, which, for most people, seems to have a fairly intuitive "point and go" feel from the start. Now, imagine a vehicle with many, many tracks, each needing individual attention with regard to speed and intended direction, and I think you have a reasonable analogy to "steering" an organization. Smaller organizations tend to form their own "communal" Engines. The whole thing is more like a collection of "hives" of Engines. Since the only real input you have is information, you must realize that "steering" is more properly described as "influencing." No matter what value the organization places on obedience, at some level individuals must still make independent decisions. Their ability to align those decisions with the best interests and direction of the company reflects the organization's ability to teach vision, mission, and values to its members. Consider this previously asked question again as well: How quickly and/or effectively will people act on information that they do not trust, or directions from people they neither trust nor respect? Use a little introspection to answer that question, and I am certain you will see that cycle time, efficiency, and quality are all at risk under such conditions.

Steering, then, is a bit problematic. Speed depends as much on successful steering as anything, but it also may be affected by the ability to maintain a sense of urgency. This is also a delicate matter, as pushing that button too hard may result in outright fear, usually with damaging effects on the steering, thus affecting the speed . . . (I will spend the whole of Chapter 8 talking about the effects of fear on the Engine, so I will suspend further comment on this particular dynamic.) Seeking excellence should provide some of your urgency; the realities of competition are probably sufficient for the rest.

Keep smooth. Keep steady. Keep focused on the vision. Reward successes. Learn from failures. Strive for learning and improvement with the rigor of an athlete pursuing faster and farther. Feed your members the best information you can give them, so every decision they make makes you better than your competition.

Fuel and Economy

There are actually three components to Improvement Engine fuel: information, motivation, and people (or at least their abilities to think and act). You might note that motivation and people have direct effects on each other as well as acting as fuel. Starving the Engine of any one of these components, or providing it in an inferior manner, will result in poor performance up to and including failure. Restricted information flow will result in fewer ideas, thus fewer and poorer decisions and actions. The effects of an absence of motivation are probably self-explanatory. People may be an issue if you simply don't have enough or if they have been poorly trained or, worse yet, poorly chosen and placed.

Too much of any of these may also have bad effects. Too much information, especially if a high percentage is irrelevant, can paralyze decision making. Too much motivation wears out some of your most important moving parts: people. Again, that button must be delicately manipulated. Having people in excess of the need builds simple inertia (e.g., from the weight of all those bloated salaries), thus slowing the Engine. Also, having people around with not enough to do is generally a bit de-motivating (there goes that people/motivation interaction again).

Luckily, information and motivation are generally cheap, at least in relative terms. The quality of both deserves serious attention, but it really doesn't matter, at least in financial terms, how much you use—as long as you don't flood the Engine. In the case of information in particular, more is better right up to the squeaking point, as long as it's relevant. People are, obviously, your major economy concern in terms of quantity, since most need compensation. Use them sparingly, but do not let their number be insufficient to the activity level or information-processing level required. You may take some relief from knowing that compensation does provide some degree of motivation, so you are helping yourself in that area. Oddly enough, you can get very good people in many cases for not much more, if anything, than people who are not good. It is wise to be very careful in your choosing, but it can be hard to tell the difference. You are advised to pay attention to this as a continual learning matter for your organization.

I have been a bit short with several very important topics in the last paragraph, and I would like to pause to point out that they are indeed, important. Employee selection, compensation, and motivation are vital activities at the very core of a company's success. This book frankly assumes you've got that under control—or, more accurately, that you will use the principles put forth in this book to devise your own means for getting them under control.

On the Road

Are you ready for a real trip, then? Something more than just a spin around the block? If so, there are a few decisions to be made:

1) Where do you want to go?
2) Why do you want to go there?
3) What roads will you take?
4) How much time do you want to take?

These questions correspond to the need for an organization to have clear, well-understood vision, mission, values, and goals. As the saying goes, "If you don't know where you want to go, any road will do to get you there." Vision and mission address the first two questions, and question 2 connects to values. Goals are the subject of questions 3 and 4; any map will show you that there are usually lots of ways to get to point B from any point A. The selection of roads depends on quite a few factors. Consider the following questions:

• Is your purpose simply to get there in the fastest and most economical way? If that were true of a trip in your car, then you would likely want to stay on major freeways, departing from them only to refuel and eat.

- What do you want to see on the way? The fastest and most direct roads are seldom the most interesting.

If your organization is seeking competitive advantage primarily by maximizing operational efficiency, then you are probably mostly working in the mode suggested by the first question. Success in this mode comes from relentless attention to cost, quality, profit margins, and basic productivity measures. You correspond most closely to the long-haul trucker, who seeks the most cost-efficient means and most profitable cargo. If, on the other hand, your organization is more driven by innovation and creating value to customers, you may be more like a tour bus driver. You have a destination and probably a date when you must be there, but the journey itself is part of the goal. In truck driver mode, you face strong competition on small margins. Everybody knows the main roads, and you generally have few alternative routes. Your advantage will come not from selecting the best goals but by pursuing the same goals as many others in a more cost-effective manner. You are likely to see large volumes as a key to success, since margins are likely to be small. In tour bus driver mode, your challenge is to find the best things to see and the best ways to make the trip comfortable, educational, and/or entertaining. Your choice of roads (goals) becomes absolutely critical, and your ability to find the less-traveled ones and highlight their attractions may be a key to success.

Most organizations must operate in both of these modes to some degree, but the balance of the two can vary to almost polar extremes. Wal-Mart is probably a pretty good example of one of those poles, driven by a consuming focus on final cost to the customer. At the other pole you might find universities or churches, where the focus on operating details is almost completely subservient to the pursuit of learning or the advancement of faith. Neither type can survive solely in one mode. Wal-Mart can't just stop looking at "road maps"; without occasional exploration of the "less-traveled" roads, they will inevitably face an unpleasant surprise from somebody who has found an advantage on one of those roads. M.I.T. and the Catholic Church can't afford to simply ignore overhead costs, since failure in that arena will disable them in the pursuit of their mission. Organizations can do one thing in this respect that is completely outside the truck vs. tour bus analogy. They can divide. A sub-portion of the organization can be split off and assigned to investigate some of those side roads.

Here is another question that will affect your "driving": What value do you place on driver and passenger safety, safety of other drivers, adherence to rules of the road, and minimizing vehicle wear? Another way of asking this, in an organizational sense, is "What are your values and what risks do they allow?" It is easy to say, in a knee-jerk response, that these are all critical, perhaps even sacred. (By the way, the only way to eliminate the risks is to never get on the road in the first place, and that really isn't even an option.) In practice, however, it is obvious that they are subject to some judgment. Let's start with safety, and let's equate it with job security. Organizations must frequently take financial risks in order to build capacity, open new markets, etc. These risks, should they result in failure, can jeopardize the security of employees at all levels. When success is the outcome, of course, all will benefit. Obviously, then, some risks will have to be taken. In the event of an "accident," though, will there be air bags for the driver (leaders/executive) only, or will passengers (lower level employees) have protection as well? Let's move on to other drivers. Some are your competition, some may be part of your "convoy" (e.g., supplier "partners"), and some are just using the same road in pursuit of things quite unrelated to you. What are you willing to do to beat the competition? Can the members of your "convoy" depend on you for support, and to what extent? Is your "driving" so aggressive that everybody on the road is at risk? Conversely, are you so timid as to create risks for yourself and others? As you see, there has to be judgment, informed by values, in making these decisions. You can't let your competition simply run past you, and you shouldn't be trying to run them off the road, either. You just want to beat them, not kill them. (I realize that some companies do, in fact, want to eliminate competitors. I merely propose that superior performance is an ethically better mechanism for accomplishing that than actual attack.

I would apply this same logic to political campaigning as well.) You want to provide support to other organizations that enable your success ("convoy" members), but that support can't and shouldn't be absolute and unconditional. Some of those organizations will fail because of their own incapabilities and misfortunes; when that happens, you shouldn't let them drag you with them. As for all those other drivers, they certainly deserve a safe place on the road. Given that your very presence on the road increases risk, how much attention will you give to ensuring the safety of all? This leads to the next point on rules of the road. I think the best anybody expects on the real road is a certain degree of predictability. In a business sense, all roads are like German autobahns; there is no speed limit. That limit is determined by your vehicle's ability to perform and enabled by the adherence of all drivers to a few rules (call them "ethics") that keep their actions somewhat predictable (e.g., slower drivers stay furthest from the median). Your organization can go as fast as it wants, but it shouldn't be reckless. Where is the dividing line? Again, that is a matter of judgment. Part of the answer is in the capabilities of the car; an equally significant portion of the answer is in the capabilities of the driver. Finally, there is the matter of wear and tear on the vehicle itself. How hard you can push your organization depends, again, on judgment and balance of various concerns. To a degree, organizations respond to a certain amount of push with not only better performance, but better endurance as well. Like some highly tuned race cars, they need to be driven fast in order to continue running well. At some point, however, this phenomenon reaches a tipping point. After this point, more failures occur, and more maintenance will be required. Running faster and harder than is good for your members may be absolutely imperative for your organization. If that's the case, you should expect and be prepared to deal with the consequences. Ultimately, if you run too fast and too hard for too long, you can be assured that there will be a catastrophic failure.

You may feel that this last section has not provided you with clear answers about how to "drive" your Improvement Engine-powered organization. This is because there are no clear answers. Just as with automobiles, every decision requires a balance of multiple factors, and no single principle will serve to guide those decisions. "Keep your eyes on the road" may sound like a good universal idea for driving, but following that rule exclusively means never looking at the dashboard. "Get there as fast as possible" maximizes a certain type of success, but an obsession with that idea can endanger others, inflict damage and wear on your vehicle, and keep you from exploring new roads. Good driving results from the driver's ability to know the destination, plan a good route, adapt to changing conditions, anticipate potential threats, stay within the rules of the road, maintain concern for the safety of passengers as well as other drivers, and keep awareness of the car's performance and indications that maintenance may be required. It's a lot to do, but ignorance of any piece can be—and usually eventually is—disastrous.

In the Pits

No matter how well you drive, things wear out and break. Engines need to be adjusted as settings and performance characteristics vary. When things in an organization break, however, fixing them can be especially complicated. There is an old joke that illustrates this issue well:

A doctor and an auto mechanic meet in a bar. Eventually, conversation turns to their professions, and the mechanic, upon learning that his drinking partner is a doctor, says, "Hey, Doc—my job is a lot like yours. We both work on fixing things inside our patients. Heck, if you look at it, an engine overhaul is a lot like open heart surgery."

The doctor thinks for a moment, then replies, "Yes, but there is one important difference. You don't have to keep your patients running while you work on them."

Organizations can't just be pulled over under a handy shade tree while you ponder what might be wrong and do actual repair work. It has previously been noted that the Improvement Engine is always running.

If you actually "stop" an organization, it will usually result in a terminal failure. Without motion and direction (activity and purpose), the organization cannot support or motivate its members. Competition will pass you by, and indeed, the traffic may be so thick and fast by the time you are ready to move again that you cannot even get back on the road.

The first key to fixing things, then, is to anticipate what is likely to fail and to make adjustments to prevent that failure. In a car, the dashboard helps provide part of this capability. The other part comes from the senses: noticing a pull to the right or left while braking, noticing a hesitation when the accelerator is pressed, etc. These same kinds of indicators are present in an organization. The "dashboard" of your organization is an assembly of key metrics, which may be somewhat different from one group to another. Some of the typical indicators here might be revenue, stock price, number of employees, profit margin, basic productivity/quality indicators, accounts receivable/payable, etc. Note that these are fairly straightforward, measurable items, akin to the readings from dashboard meters. Less straightforward might be factors such as morale, validity of purpose, adequacy of goals, and correctness of knowledge and assumptions. How does a driver quantify the sense that a car "just doesn't have the same zip?" When a car does start to pull during braking, how acute are the senses that allow the earliest awareness of that change? The ability to know these things is critical to good performance in a car. In an organization, I would maintain they are at least as critical, if not more.

In most cases, the drivers of an organization (executives and managers) must perform their own maintenance. As I said before, the organization can't be stopped for repairs. Also, there is no separate group to do such repairs; organizations look to their leaders for both operational and remedial direction. Finally, as also previously noted, the Improvement Engine's performance is directly related to how well it receives guidance; steering and speed are inseparable, unlike a car.

The Improvement Engine diagram can be used as a simple analytical tool to trace the reasons for both quantifiable and somewhat intangible changes in performance. Just consider your problem, look at the diagram, and point to the place where things went wrong. The quantifiable changes are mostly found within the "Invent" and "Apply" boxes. The results of activities within those boxes are mostly (though not entirely) empirically understandable, although it should be remembered that the measurable result may have an intangible cause. Other factors affecting performance, such as the effects of new knowledge and of trust and respect within and across groups, are less measurable, as are the effects of varying levels of quality associated with decisions made in the center box (improvement/learning strategies). Once you have pointed to the place where things went wrong, ask yourself if that is where the problem started or just where it became visible. Did productivity drop (as measurable in the "Apply" box) because of a hard-to-produce design? Was the quality of the design (as measurable in the "Invent" box) less than it should have been because of a failure in providing information on production capabilities or customer expectations? Finally, ask yourself—in the most honest way possible—what levels of trust and respect may have had to do with contributing to the failure. Then ask yourself how the failure itself has affected ongoing levels of trust and respect (this will allow you to get on the proactive side of dealing with the issue). By the way, I notice that I have assumed you are using the diagram to analyze a problem/failure. Let's face it, that's what we spend a lot of time doing, and it is certainly the most likely first use you will make of the model. It should be noted and even emphasized, however, that you may just as well use the Engine model to analyze successes. It will tell you as much about what may have gone right as what went wrong.

I would also emphasize the roles of sensitivity, intuition, and introspection in using the Engine successfully as a failure/success analysis tool. You have heard of "horse whisperers"—people who use a very calm, empathetic approach to horse training that takes advantage of the horse's own natural communication devices. Maybe there are "organization whisperers"—people who can almost mystically note and define the signals that reveal the well-being of groups of people. Perhaps participative management, with its focus on "soft" skills, reflects the dawn of an age of such "whisperers." Of one thing I am certain: these things have an effect on organizational systems, and if they are ignored, they are as likely as any other cause to be the ultimate downfall of an organization. At some point, if trust and respect within an organization are low enough, it ceases to be a real organization. It becomes instead a collection of individuals showing outward compliance to direction while actually protecting their individual interests above all else. At some point, if lack of trust and respect are disabling the capacity of your organization to improve, you are probably best advised to blame everybody equally (since they all had a hand in it), declare an immediate amnesty, and hope that old grudges can be forgiven quickly enough to avoid Chapter 11.

Faster

Some time around the turn of the last century, there was an occasion when two of the earliest drivers met in the same location with two of the earliest cars. I would be willing to bet that on that same day the automobile race was invented. There is an undeniable tendency for humans to want to make things go faster and to find out whose thing is fastest. The same is true for organizations; they all want to know how to go as fast as they can. While there is sometimes danger and risk involved, the underlying motives are often best characterized as curiosity and a striving for excellence. As in many endeavors, those who have pushed the envelope in racing cars, and incurred great danger and risk in doing so, have contributed knowledge that has improved both the performance and safety of regular vehicles.

If you are looking to get truly exceptional performance from your Improvement Engine, what should you do? If you asked that question about your car at your local high-performance auto shop, you would get a reasonably concise list of factors that are the main starting points. The first three can be affected with equipment changes that don't require rebuilding your engine

- Carburetion—maximize the amount and flammability of fuel going into your engine up to the point where all delivered fuel can be burned
- Exhaust—make sure your engine breathes in and out freely
- Ignition—deliver a powerful, controlled spark to ignite your fuel, and burn all of the fuel delivered

If you are willing to undergo more substantial modifications, the shop might recommend changes in two other factors:

- Camshaft—optimize the opening and closing of valves, and thus the delivery and mixing of air and fuel, by modifications to the camshaft
- Compression—decrease the space where fuel is ignited so that the resulting explosion is more powerful and drives the piston faster

If you do enough of these things, and if you actually plan to drive your vehicle in accordance with its new capabilities, you might be well advised to do things to tires, steering, brakes and suspension, so that you will be able to handle the increased speeds safely and effectively. When dealing with an Improvement Engine, however, handling is a function of Engine performance, so we will focus our attention on the changes which, in a car, are relative to the engine itself. Remember that the most efficient operation of the Engine is a balancing act of several factors. No single knob—not even the trust and respect knobs—can simply be maximized in order to improve performance. (More on this in the next "What to Do" chapter. Also, in the "Data and Validation" chapter, note that trust-building for trust's sake, without commitment to mutual objectives is a generally pointless pursuit.)

Carburetion

Information is the fuel for the Improvement Engine. In general, you want to deliver all you can burn and burn all you deliver. At the edges of high performance, this becomes a close balancing act. You want lots of information to get to your people, but you must not overload them. There is a cliff in the graph of knowledge input versus performance. Up to a point, performance increases with the amount of knowledge provided. When that point is reached, however, and people are overloaded with information, performance deteriorates rapidly. If decision making becomes paralyzed, it also paralyzes action at that level and all below it.

Quality of information is also a huge consideration. In high-performance vehicles, special fuels are used which allow for faster and more complete burning. Make sure your organization gets good information. Supply people with journals that keep them posted on new developments in their fields. Attend conferences where the best knowledge about your type of business is discussed. Encourage continuing education.

As the Improvement Engine diagram reveals, trust and respect will act as carburetion devices; at least they will certainly have an effect on the speed of information flow and the nature of information transferred. People will act more quickly and with more energy on information from sources they trust. They will deliver information more readily and honestly to those from whom they have a sense of respect.

Exhaust

In an Improvement Engine, trust and respect also serve the exhaust function. Every piece of information delivered or received is gated by these factors. In an automobile, turbochargers are used to push more and more air (and thus more flame-enabling oxygen) into the engine. The more oxygen available, the more fuel can be burned. While it is possible to deliver too much air to an automobile engine, you can compensate by delivering more fuel, again up to the point of flooding the engine.

Essentially, if you maintain a correct balance between fuel and air delivery, you can continue to maximize both until the capacity of the piston chamber to contain the explosion is reached. Correspondingly, in an Improvement Engine, it is usually difficult to create too much trust and respect. As they increase, they simply allow more information to be shared and processed, and the outcome continues to be higher performance. Remember that simply maximizing them is not a valid goal, however. There are, in fact, places in every process where trust levels should remain low, in a sense. These are the places where prudence and caution *should* be applied, where risks *are* high, where controls *must* be rigorous. The trick in such cases is to establish the optimal level of trust. (More on this in the discussion of the "optimal bureaucracy" in Chapter 11.)

Ignition

People are the igniters in the Improvement. Information is the fuel, and trust and respect enable the flow of fuel and air, but the "spark" comes from the human brain. Initiative is the prerogative of people. What can you do to maximize the spark? Keep the organization curious. Show that you value imagination and creativity as well as dedication and energetic execution. Make sure people are always learning and have immediate opportunities to apply that learning.

Camshaft

As I said above, camshaft modifications are a bit more ambitious than changes in the previous three categories. If you want to actually pursue a modification of this level, I would say it would require installing resources dedicated to the pre-processing of information for the rest of the organization. This would mean creating a group whose purpose is to obtain, screen, and summarize the best and most powerful information for your specific needs. In many organizations, this function is referred to as Research and Development. Too often, however, such groups are limited in their activities to technical development. Every major company has many more functions than are reflected in its specialty. At a minimum, every company must deal with basic financial and human relations issues. I have seen few companies, however, who have actively dedicated resources to improving their people through advanced HR practices. (I have seen several who *think* they are doing so, though. Such efforts often simply become "program of the moment" efforts, usually because they were never taken seriously by management in the first place.) Making a conscious organizational effort to pursue advanced knowledge in all operations can set you apart from your competition.

Compression

If there is a way to achieve higher compression in the Improvement Engine, it would be through structuring facilities and events so that knowledge, creativity, and energy are channeled into opportunities to make faster and more powerful decisions. Again, these purposes might require significant changes in your organization. Changing the physical layout of a facility or rearranging office assignments along lines other than the traditional ones of hierarchy and group proximity can be expensive, and they may even be threatening to some. Doing so without careful research, forethought, and planning will disrupt lines of communication currently feeding existing channels of learning and improvement. I emphasize that such changes, while possibly productive, are major modifications to your Engine and will require significant, long-term attention in order to be successful.

Similarly, the use of professional facilitators to design and lead meetings in more creative and focused ways is a logical strategy to increase "compression." These same changes, however, may be seen as expensive and/or threatening by some, especially where meetings are viewed as key leadership demonstration opportunities. The results, however, can be extraordinary. The potential downside, as with changes to knowledge processing discussed in the camshaft section, is in letting these become temporary and meaningless programs. If the decision making culture is to be changed successfully, those changes must be reflected consistently right to the top of the organization.

Reflection:

- The main point of this whole chapter has been to introduce trust and respect as gating factors to each element of the Improvement Engine—and to thus explain the "human" rationale of continuous improvement.

  - What is the state of trust and respect in your organization? If you were to look for specific evidence of them, what would you find, good and bad?
  - Does your organization have stated vision, mission, and values, and are they clearly understood by the members? Are members reasonably "safe" in taking independent action as long as such action is clearly in support of the vision/mission and in accordance with values?
  - How do structures and systems within your organization support or disable trust and respect? (Consider especially systems for evaluating human performance and approving expenditures.)
  - How do groups within your organization interact? Are there groups with a known history of mutual suspicion?
  - How do your executives interact? Are they visibly in support of each other, or are they visibly in competition with each other?

- The simplest way for people to learn to trust each other is to see each other make commitments to do things in support of the other and then to see those commitments kept.—in other words, to see that they can rely on others to do what they say they will do.

- What can be done in your organization to create simple, visible ways for individuals and groups to make and keep commitments with each other, starting small and getting progressively bigger?
- How well does your basic organizational culture reflect a valuing of making and keeping commitments? (Start with the concept of "on time." Do meetings start on time? Are appointments consistently kept? Are assignments routinely completed on schedule? Behaviors in each of these areas can send signals that reflect on the organization's commitment to commitment itself.)

- Use the Improvement Engine diagram as a visual prompt to trace reasons for failure and success.

  - (If you didn't already do this at the start of the book . . .) Make a list of three major initiatives that have gone well. Then make a list of three major initiatives that have not gone well. Look at the Engine diagram, and trace each event through its invention and application. In each case, take a close look at the degree to which trust and respect issues were enablers of success or failure, and consider what actions might have been taken to remediate negative issues in advance.
  - Look at a current plan of action for your organization. Are there places where trust and respect issues might put the plan at risk? How can trust be built in advance to reduce risk?

- Remember that we do not simply "belong" on one side of the Engine or another by virtue of the name of our department. Not only do we frequently find ourselves changing positions as we go from one activity to another, we also can make that switch in the course of a single interaction, as the sales agent goes from listening to needs (applying input) to proposing (innovating) solutions.

- Just think about that . . .

• Trust is a huge factor, but it is not the universal "knob" for running your organization's Improvement Engine. You need processes, structure, and broad involvement in decision making. The reasons *why* these things work, though, will still—ironically—come back to trust, as *people* must always and finally make the choices about how—or even whether—to act. Trust is more than a "people skill"; it is integral to process design and control.

- Just think about that, too . . .

Chapter 7

The Eighth Point

"Now is the time to understand more, so that we may fear less."

Marie Curie

In his book <u>Out of the Crisis</u>, Dr. W. Edwards Deming put forth 14 points as the principles of his philosophy on continuous improvement and business management in general. Specifically, he referred to these as the principles which management must act upon in order to accomplish the *transformation* (his word) from traditional, dysfunctional systems to efficient, quality-oriented organizations. I have reviewed these principles and their application to the Improvement Engine in the previous chapter. One of those points, however, I postponed for further discussion. It is time for that discussion.

To begin that discussion, let me call your attention again to the Case of the Vomiting Manager from Chapter 7. You may remember he faced an Operations Review in front of a notoriously abusive director on a month of poor performance. That man was afraid. In fact, "terrified" might be a better description. He was no coward; he was prepared to march bravely to the doom that awaited him. (In my personal view of the world, a person without fear is a fool, as there are, in fact, things worth fearing; a person who overcomes fear to take action is a hero.) In addition, he had done the best he could to point blame away from people he valued. In military situations, these behaviors are called "courage" and "watching out for your buddies." Some of the blame he was prepared to take himself, even though his subordinates probably deserved some share of responsibility for that month's performance. As much as possible, he diverted blame toward inanimate things: business conditions, equipment issues, organizational disconnects, etc. Where he felt he had to, he pointed some fingers at other groups. In doing that, he tried to prioritize those with which he usually had antagonistic relationships. The presentation, though it could not help but reflect poor overall results, deflected attention as much as possible from any points that might have incurred even more humiliating wrath from the director. Given the motives behind the creation of the presentation, it should be no wonder that it contained an inordinate number of deceptions and half-truths—and some outright lies. The production manager had spent many hours over several days—more than four times the usual time devoted to this task, much of it after normal work hours—massaging it to its final state. Based on the lack of truth involved, there was no hope that the organization could learn anything from the exchange of information about to ensue in that review. Perhaps most pointedly, this manager's chief learning from this experience was, in the future, to keep close track of and document the failures of those whom he wished to blame. (He and I talked about it later, that's how I know all this.) This learning vastly overshadowed anything he might have learned about how to prevent a recurrence of the poor performance itself. After all, he knew that eventually, no matter what he learned or did, another poor month would come his way—they always do—and his top priority now was to be ready to defend himself when it did.

The Engine was running—but to what purpose and in what direction?

The point of Deming's which I deferred for later discussion was his eighth point: "Drive out fear". This one gets a tremendous amount of debate. The discussions include comments/questions like the following:

"Isn't a little fear a good thing? It sharpens the mind."

"Surely he doesn't mean *all* fear . . ."

"How can you have any discipline if there isn't any fear of consequences?"

(This is my personal favorite) "What do you think he *really* meant by that?"

I'm pretty sure I know what he really meant, which is just what he said, and I think all these questions are ways of diverting attention from an uncomfortable reality: a lot of us believe fear is an effective tool, and we are comfortable using it because we often see immediate results from it. Many of us, however, are uncomfortable admitting this openly because it sounds bad, even to our own ears. After all, especially in the modern political environment, and especially in post-9/11 America, we face an uncomfortable moral issue: using fear to get people to do what you want is generally called "terrorism" these days. (Pardon a bit of hyperbole on my part, but the point is real.) Thus we couch our use of fear in terms like "making clear the consequences of adverse behavior or results," or "elevating the level of concern." For the most part, I regard these as euphemisms and shabby excuses.

The operation of fear in the Physics of Success and on the Improvement Engine is complex. There are four fundamental points that I would make about the interactions involved. The use of fear and intimidation, especially as management or "leadership" tools, has the following drawbacks:

1) Fear misdirects learning and improvement, thus diverting the Engine's energy to unproductive pursuits.
2) As a motivator, fear is more volatile, less predictable, and therefore riskier than kindness or, at least, emotional objectivity.
3) "Leadership" by fear is simply less effective and therefore less successful in most circumstances, especially in the long run.
4) Using fear to drive people's behavior is based on an inferior moral principle—and people know it.

(Note that I put leadership in quotes above when it was linked to fear. This is because I believe that fear can only accomplish a form of management, not leadership. The concept of "management" is based on establishing and maintaining control; fear can accomplish this, at least to some degree. I object in principle, however, to calling this "leadership." I would also point out that Dr. Deming makes this exact same distinction.)

Consider the following point, which will inform the entire discussion on fear. Trust, predictability, and fear are all closely interrelated. If a person, process, or product is unpredictable, that is tantamount to saying that it cannot be trusted. Our concept of trusting something is closely linked to the idea that we have a relatively reliable understanding of future probabilities in our interaction with that thing. In personal relationships, a person whose behavior is not predictable is considered "unreliable"—not to be trusted. If we are uncertain about the likelihood that our car will operate as expected tomorrow, we cease to trust in it as our means of transportation. All of this is closely linked to the fact that we fear what we cannot predict, for what we cannot predict we cannot control. Loss of control is a great, often unidentified source of fear for humans. Our success as a species, however, has come from exactly the fact that, to a higher degree than any other species, we are capable of exerting a remarkable amount of control over our environment. We build houses to control the impact of exposure to the elements. We raise crops and animals to make our access to food more reliable. We invest in retirement plans to assure that our later years, when we are tired from a lifetime of work, may still be comfortable without a source of income directly from our current efforts. In short, we go to extensive lengths to make our lives predictable. This expectation of control even has its darker side, especially as aspects of controlling the behavior of others are concerned. The person whom we label a "control freak" is, in fact, a person reacting to his or her own fear of not having a predictable environment. All three concepts, then, are related. We fear what we cannot predict. We do not trust that which has a low level of predictability, and we certainly do not trust that which we fear. Lack of trust is both a manifestation of, and a creator of, fear of the unknown and unknowable—the unpredictable.

In order to fully comprehend the impact of fear, we need to change our emotional response to the word. As modern business thinking has redefined the term "value," we also need to redefine "fear." Whenever I teach the concept of "value," as it has been redefined in the last few decades, I always meet some resistance. In particular, people are most frequently reluctant to abandon the idea that inspection adds value. As I previously pointed out, it does not meet the first criterion of this new "value" definition, since inspection does not actually change the thing inspected. At best, inspection may reveal some fixable problem, but then fixing it fails a second criterion of "value"; it was not done right the first time, and so you now have two consecutive non-value-added activities. In the Lean world, this is also called "waste." And yet they argue that inspection adds value; they learn to improve our products, they keep defective products out of the customer's hands. I point out that the only reason they do inspections is because they sometimes do things wrong; you would never need inspection of a process that always performs perfectly. Still they argue. I point out that it is perfectly legitimate—even necessary—to perform a lot of non-value-added functions (e.g., Payroll, Quality, Facilities, etc.) in order to keep a company running. These even have names in the Lean language like "non-value-added but necessary," and "internal business value." Still they argue. Why? I have conclusively proven that inspection does not meet the definition of value, haven't I?

The problem here is that they haven't truly adopted the new definition. People have emotional meanings—connotations—for some words that are difficult to change. It is emotionally challenging for many to make such changes. It is difficult for them to see with new eyes what "waste" and "value" really are in this new context. It may be very difficult to acknowledge that perhaps 70-80% of what their organization does falls under the term "non-value-added." (By the way, that's not abnormal for most organizations.) It may be close to impossible to acknowledge that their entire job—perhaps their entire career—is dedicated to something with an impotent, embarrassing term like "non-value-added." Therein lies the problem: fear of embarrassment. Another obvious emotional problem with the new definition is how that term might affect current and future employment prospects. After all, if your function is "non-value-added" and the product of all your efforts is "waste," how valuable are you to the company? Are you part of that "necessary" group? Just how necessary is "necessary" anyway, when the going gets tough? By redefining this term, we introduce the fear of redundancy, which threatens jobs, which threatens income, which threatens survival . . . No wonder people struggle with this definition. Yet the definition has merit. It does open new eyes on the world. It helps us identify opportunity.

Here, then is fear in its "new" definition: *Fear is the simple acknowledgement of threat.* That's all. The way we react to fear is another matter. (Note the "Doubt and Dread" path described below.) We have a lot of emotional baggage around this word as well, probably a lot more than we do with "value." Fear—as we understand it emotionally—has the tendency to be regarded as cowardice and therefore shameful. No one wants to admit to being "afraid." If you look at the "new" definition above, though, there is nothing to be ashamed of. Acknowledging that something is a threat is often a good thing, especially if it actually is one. The very concepts of caution, prudence, and due diligence come from this acknowledgement. All of them are protections we establish against often perfectly justifiable fears.

Perhaps you believe there is no or little evidence of fear in your organization. If so, look at the definition again. Do you do inspections and put process controls in place? Do certain decisions and transactions require multiple approvals? Do you exercise due diligence? All of these are manifestations of fear, if you use the "new" definition. We recognize the threat of errors and the danger of decisions without oversight. History has taught us, well and accurately, that these things do happen. They are legitimate threats, and we "fear" them. Our reaction is to gain control over them (note the earlier discussion about our fear of loss of control), which usually generates "non-value-added" activities. Here is a thinking point for Lean: How much "waste" (in its new definition) is due to "fear" (likewise in its new definition)?

Fear and Learning:

Let's look at what fear does to learning and improvement. From the Physics, we know that learning and change must be combined to achieve improvement. There is a reality associated with this which I have previously not discussed, however. All changes—even the most positive ones—induce at least a little fear. Change almost always interferes with comfort, which is a major component of happiness, and we certainly fear any disruption of our happiness. We react to this fear in one of two ways: either we take the path of faith and hope to combat the fear, or we follow a path of doubt and dread, allowing the fear to be preeminent in guiding us. Either of these paths may be followed to varying degrees; it is not a case of all or nothing. The nature of the change and the concern it arouses are factors, as is the individual's sensitivity. The threats and opportunities facing the organization involved create an atmosphere likely to influence the choice of paths and the level of emotion, as does the culture of the organization itself. Words like "hope" and "dread" imply fairly high levels of emotion. In many, if not most, cases these words are a bit extreme considering the real level of emotion involved. I use them purposely as reminders of the most extreme possibilities.

If we follow the path of faith and hope up the ladder of equations that form the Physics of Success, we often see something like the following sequence, which is a path based on principle:

1) We approach **Change** with courage. Despite fears and misgivings, we look to what Change will accomplish for us and how our world will be better for it.

2) We pursue **Improvement** with confidence. Faith makes us believe both that we can accomplish what we have set out to do and that the result will be to our benefit. We allow Vision to inspire us toward Progress.

3) We validate our accomplishment, which allows us to attach trust to **Progress**. We believe that what we have accomplished is a real benefit, not a contrived one.

4) We achieve **Success** with satisfaction and pride. At the end of it all, we regain a level of comfort and look back on what we have done with a real sense of it having been worth it.

If, on the other hand, if we follow the path of doubt and dread, we are apt to see the following, which is more of a "means to an end" path:

1) We approach **Change** with frustration. Having no confidence that Change will be accomplished—or that if it is, no real benefit will result—we allow our (probably justified) fears to color required actions as a nuisance. We prepare for disappointment.

2) We pursue **Improvement** with anger. There is a need for strong emotion to drive actions in the face of change—to get us past the inertia of doubt. In the absence of faith and hope, we frequently use anger to help get us moving in this case.

3) We attach suspicion and self-deception to (alleged) **Progress**. Since we fear the change and its outcomes, we do not examine them too closely. On the surface, we may claim accomplishment, but we privately suspect the claim.

4) We achieve (alleged) **Success** in a paradoxical state of exhaustion and arrogance. Sensing no real victory, we feel only the toll that the effort has taken on us. Because we cannot emotionally afford to really believe that it was all a waste, we shout down all disclaimers.

A graphic representation of these paths might look like this:

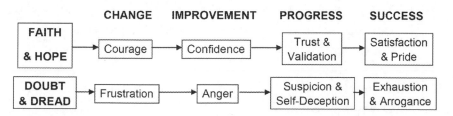

127

Actually, the path of doubt and dread may be a little more complex, as it also diverts into two paths. People react to fear in one of two ways, depending again on factors like the level of threat perceived, personal experience, prevailing organizational culture, etc. Often they are swept on from frustration to anger, as this is a good emotional defense mechanism that allows one to retain at least a semblance of pride. Other conditions, however, lead to confusion and uncertainty and an inability to choose either an emotional or action-based response.

If anger is the primary reaction, there is a predictable set of consequences:

1) Anger will damage trust. This results in emotions and actions that are distractions; people divert energy to self-defense mechanisms and deceptions instead of learning and improvement (reference the Case of the Vomiting Manager.) All of this adds no value and reduces productivity.

2) When anger is our driver, we tend to attack. Attack is a means for destruction, and destruction is seldom productive.

3) As the above graphic indicates, the anger/attack approach often leads to a point of self-deception. We must justify what we know to have been less-than-admirable emotions or actions, so we deceive ourselves into believing that they were necessary (ends justify the means). This stance often creates polarity issues between those who acted and those who were affected. The affected are resentful of the damage done; the actors are self-righteous about the need to have done it. The real tragedy here, in terms of the Improvement Engine, is the loss of sight involved. Both the resentful and the self-righteous are at the top of the Ladder of Inference, acting on beliefs without examination. Neither group can now see the real data that might create learning. The organization's horizon becomes shortened, as Vision is impaired by an unwillingness to see.

The other reaction to fear has equally predictable—and equally unproductive—consequences:

1) Instead of getting angry because of fear, people simply get confused. They recognize the threat, but they are uncertain about how to respond. Even small threats may seem to them to have severe or unbearable consequences, and they fear making the wrong choice. Indecision and uncertainty slow down the organization. Productivity drops.

2) As the threat increases, or as deadlines near, indecision turns to desperation. In this state, people go from doing nothing to doing anything they think will work to avoid the perceived consequences. In this state, Vision shortens; people typically wait until the last minute to make choices; thus they are focused entirely on short-term issues and consequences. You don't have to watch many shows about real crime to learn that people will make incredibly bad choices with respect to long-term consequences in order to avoid addressing even low-level short-term consequences. (Police chase videos offer some particularly stunning examples.) Just as obviously, making desperate, wrong choices is not likely to be a dependable path to organizational productivity.

3) The end of this path is hopelessness. Because things haven't worked before, people come to believe that nothing can or will work. The best course of action seems to be no action at all. Productivity halts. Perhaps even worse, this state of mind prevents any meaningful Vision. A person without hope cannot see past his or her immediate despair.

Updating the above graphic to reflect this split on the "doubt and dread" path gives us something like this:

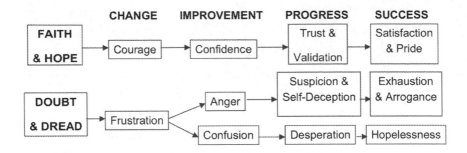

The effects of fear, then, as observed through the lens of the Physics of Success, are to:

1) heighten the likelihood of wrong choices,
2) shorten the organizational horizon, and
3) reduce productivity—or at least divert productivity toward unaligned objectives.

What does the Improvement Engine tell us about the impact of fear? You may remember the question I asked you about your reaction to untrustworthy information or sources:

- Do you take longer to act on information that you don't trust or which comes from a source you don't trust?

A similar question applies to fear:

- Do you take longer to act when you fear the consequences?

I imagine you do. There is a certain amount of fear that is useful here—enough to inspire a sense of caution proportional to the consequences, enough to inspire thorough planning and some consideration of back-up planning, enough to motivate due diligence. When fear is excessive, however, and especially when consequences imposed by the organization are perceived as disproportional to the actual consequences of a wrong decision, decision making slows unnecessarily. The level of acceptable risk lowers, and this can stifle a necessary level of creativity. When the honest mistake, the wrong guess, and the error in judgment all meet the same consequences as the incompetent blunder, the ethical lapse, or the malicious subversion, trust in the organization's judgment falters, and the guidance of its leaders becomes suspect. All of this slows both decision making and action. That, in turn, expands the cycle time of improvement, opening the window of opportunity to less fear-driven competitors.

I have used the term "horizon" rather frequently in the last discussions. I don't remember exactly when this term crept into biz-speak popularity, but I like it. It perfectly describes a characteristic which, I believe, is a primary component in determining likelihood of success. Quite simply, it refers to the length of time the organization is looking forward in planning today's actions. Long-term success can only come from a view of a distant horizon.

I have shown the impact of horizon in the Physics of success; it impacts Vision, which helps direct Progress. Its effect on the Improvement Engine is a bit subtle, however, and it is relative to the workings of the Ladder of Inference. You may remember that the "reflexive loop" in the Ladder actually affects the future selection of data, screening out some of what is, in fact, actually happening. That loop is affected by fear. Fear doesn't operate well in the long term. We tend to shrug off fears of long-term consequences, believing they are unproductive. Such consequences are, after all, often easily avoidable as long as they are understood, or they are completely unavoidable—"destiny"—and so do not benefit from any particular planning. Short-term fears, however, with immediate, impending consequences, get our full attention. They cause us to focus only on the data and experience that we believe can help us avoid disaster. We screen out the data relating to long-term issues. Our horizon shortens.

This means that, under these conditions, the information feeding the Improvement Engine is all based on short-term issues as well. Improvement efforts can only focus on the information available, and if the level of fear in the organization has screened out all but the data relating to immediate threats, then the only improvements will be short-term as well. Not only that, but the decisions and actions taken may have long-term negative effects that are ignored. Again, the competitor who is less driven by fear has a window of opportunity.

You have seen this in action, haven't you? I made reference to police chase videos earlier. One of these videos I have seen frequently (it is quite dramatic) shows a couple in a truck who have just stolen a lawn mower. They run a red light at high speed. The truck they are driving seems to vanish as it is smashed by a much larger truck traveling at high speed. Both occupants of the smaller truck are killed immediately. The primary impact on the viewer is horror, but there is, honestly, also a bit of sardonic humor hanging in the background, reflecting on the idiocy and waste of the incident. Trading your life for a lawn mower reflects a significant failure in long-term planning.

You have seen it in organizations as well, though. One of its most frequent manifestations is short-term cost-cutting tactics. In response to poor business conditions and low revenue, organizations look to cost reductions that will allow them to "make the quarter." (Thoughts about making the year, or making the decade for that matter, are cast aside . . .) One of the most frequent responses I have seen is to cut training. First of all, this betrays a lot of underlying assumptions that the organization's leaders have about the value of learning; they see it as a luxury, not a necessity. (Sadly, if their learning is poorly executed—see the first four chapters of this book—they may be right.) Second, it disables at least one of the more important strategies for improving performance, which might apply to the very situation the organization is facing. The short-sightedness of this and other measures taken to achieve quarterly goals is not lost on employees, especially when these measures are obviously at the expense of long-term issues. They recognize these measures as fear-based and irrational, and their trust of the organization's judgment drops accordingly. As for the argument about meeting Wall Street's expectations, and the responsibility to shareholders to do so, I say, "Bunk." If the issue is truly just the quarter, then the next quarter will show a recovery, and the company is doing a greater disservice to its shareholders by impeding improvement than by not making the quarter. If the issue is more than just the quarter, then the company should be dealing more openly with its shareholders about the larger problem. As for Wall Street, well, it needs to learn these lessons as well. If companies ceased pandering to the short-term expectations of Wall Street and focused instead on making progress as fast as possible, then it would rapidly become apparent that "making the quarter" every quarter might not be the most reliable indicator of a successful investment. Ultimately, making money wins on Wall Street. If successful companies are eventually determined to be profitable investments based more on their long-range prospects than on their performance during arbitrary, volatile, three-month periods, Wall Street will change its tune. (By the way, I have also heard of companies who take hard times as an opportunity to accelerate training, especially if the economic slump is due to external market conditions and may be reliably anticipated to improve. After all, lower demand for their products or services should mean lower demand on people's time, and that time can be productively turned to learning. These companies, in my experience, are rare.)

I have pointed out earlier that bad experience can be a good prompt for learning and that organizations should learn to examine such occasions more productively. However, bad experiences often create fears, and justifiably so. Thus there are two points which should be remembered about this concept. First, just because we may learn well from adversity, that does not mean that adversity is a particularly "good" or admirable learning tool. Nothing about these experiences inspires the learner to trust or value the "teacher," and that means that learning will be less efficient. Second, our learning from bad experience is not nearly as productive as the learning from trustworthy sources. Ultimately, fear can only teach you what *not* to do. This is learning of a sort, but note that it essentially promotes (encourages) *inaction*. How effective is *that*? In the discussion of the Physics of Success, I showed that this type of learning qualifies as Improvement, but it does not accomplish real Progress, as it is not aligned with Vision. I, at least, don't know anybody whose Vision includes the frustration and pain of this process; it focuses instead on the better state to be achieved through Improvement.

Assigning blame is also a great way to avoid learning. It sets an atmosphere of fear, and therefore distrust, around the issue. Additionally, the identification of a single fault or scapegoat (as is our usual practice, despite the fact that human processes almost always fail due to the effects of various weights of several factors) allows all but the scapegoat to walk away without feeling they may have overlooked an opportunity to improve themselves. The infection has, after all, been removed . . . hasn't it?

A final point about fear and learning: Fear slows and degrades the learning process. Ask yourself—very honestly—the following: If people fear the people to whom they give information, what is the likely effect? Lack of trust is based on fear. What does this do to the flow of information, therefore learning, and therefore the potential for improvement? If fear is present in "minor" forms such as intimidation or harassment, especially if these are tolerated or (even worse) institutionalized, the flow of information will both slow and degenerate as people divert their time to such unproductive activities as obsessing over ways to present negative information in positive ways (ranging from "spin" to outright lies) or simply avoiding "opportunities" to pass on data/information. If fear is at very high levels (e.g., due to leadership by threat, significant economic threat, physical threat, physical harm, torture, etc.) some must argue that information can be gotten from the reluctant. I admit that, in the darkest corners of my imagination, I believe I would say anything under the malicious and merciless use of pain as encouragement. (This argument as an excuse for using fear as a leadership tool does not seem rational to me, but it is the only way to explain some observed leadership behaviors.) I would also, however, try to disguise any truth divulged by throwing in more and contradictory—or at least irrelevant—information. Records of people who have been tortured in such fashion seem to confirm that the argument against getting reliable information from the tortured is valid. I would argue that such methods are inefficient, not to mention brutal. You will get the information, all right—plus a whole lot more that must be sifted for truth and judged (instead of depended upon)—for its verity and value. And should you damage or kill—well, that's just plain wasteful.

Fear and Motivation:

Motivation is a task of leadership, so much of what may be said in this section will apply to leaders. Perhaps more accurately, it will apply to those in positions of power over the behavior and/or well-being of others. Some of these may not be leaders, in point of fact; remember the distinction made above between "leadership" and "management." Fear is, without a doubt, a potentially strong motivator. What, however, are the consequences of using it in such a manner?

Let's talk first about one of the most common fear-based motivational tools/behaviors: anger. We tend to think of anger as an emotion, but it is an observable behavior as well, and we certainly use anger to influence the behavior of others. There is a known pattern of behaviors that communicate anger: raising one's voice and/or employing tones of voice that imply threat; using certain facial expressions; using threatening or abusive language; gesturing in a short, sharp manner, etc. We know these signs and can identify them even from a distance.

Anger—especially demonstrable, visible anger—is a product of fear as well as a tool intended to create fear. The second part of that statement may seem intuitive (though it may grate somewhat against our sensibilities), but the first is something we prefer not to admit. We would like to believe that when we are angry, we are justifiably lashing out at offenses. Underneath it all, however, is a simple piece of logic: we would never get angry at something unless we believed it presented a threat to something we value, and in my book, fear is just that: acknowledging the threat. What is jealous anger but the reaction to the fear of lost love? What is righteous anger but a reaction to threatened moral values? Why do we succumb so easily to "road rage" if it is not because of the threat to our property and lives that we perceive as a result of another's rash act? Anger allows us to react to fear while maintaining our pride. The other reactions to fear, like terror and timidity, are consistently viewed as shameful, so there is good reason to find another path for releasing our emotional reaction to fear.

An interesting point in all this is that we tend to attach the responsibility for anger to other people and events. We talk about people and situations "making" us angry. There is a fallacy in that phrasing. Years ago, I took some training that made the point that things just happen; our reactions to them are choices. Anger, in particular, is a choice. Nobody and nothing *makes* you angry. People do things, and other things just happen, and you *choose* anger as the reaction. Especially if the level of fear is high, and the emotional reaction is strong, we may not notice the choice; we leap into anger as a protective mechanism without realizing that any choice was made. That training class, while it made me completely re-think the process by which I came to anger, failed to supply the critical emotional link in the process: fear. Things, events, people, etc. do, in fact, *make* you afraid. Anger is a frequent response, often fueled by pride, which itself is many times an artifact of the fear of shame. Interestingly, when you focus on what fear "made" you angry (inspired your anger is more correct), *you* take responsibility for the anger. Whenever I analyze my own tendencies toward anger, I find fear at their root, and I am forced to confront that fear, to take responsibility for it instead of denying it through anger. Even more interestingly, I find I have much more of a positive effect and outcome in dealing with angry people when, instead of returning the anger in kind (I am, after all, threatened by—afraid of—their demonstration of anger, as this makes them unpredictable and therefore untrustworthy), I try to understand what fear might be acting on them and address the issues I think might be causing them to be afraid. It is a lot easier to behave sympathetically with a person you believe is afraid than it is to treat kindly a person you simply see as angry.

- Take a moment here to validate this for yourself. Think of the last time you got really angry—or even the last two or three times. In each case, was something you valued being threatened? Can you acknowledge a level of fear that provoked your anger? Does pride interfere with that self-examination? Do you find it difficult or embarrassing to think that you might have been afraid?

What does anger do when we use it to influence others? Let's start with an ugly little admission: when we use anger, we are generally trying to create fear: fear of ourselves or fear of the situation we are describing. In the former condition, use of anger implies that the people you are interacting with are responsible for your anger. In the latter, we are generally using anger to "get the attention" of our audience, get them to share the fear that causes our own anger, and, possibly, gain power or influence over them through this strategy. In parenting, anger (properly managed, I might emphasize) plays an important role. It makes our children afraid, of course, but hopefully, it makes them afraid of things they should justifiably be afraid of. Especially for smaller children, logic and reasoning will not accomplish this. Their brains are not developed enough to allow them to have accurate perceptions about the effects associated with their actions. At very early ages, they have no clue whatsoever what to be afraid of. Sometimes our own raw fear in response to their actions (e.g. trying to touch a hot burner on the kitchen range) communicates to them that they too should fear this. Sometimes (e.g. leaving the house without telling anyone) we must use anger to get our point across. The aim is to achieve a balance: the child learns to fear the things it should fear without coming to believe that the parent is one of those things. In some unfortunate cases, of course, it may be that the best learning *is* to fear the parent.

When we are grown up, however, and when logic and reasoning are sufficiently developed, what is the real effect of anger on our motivation and action, especially as we interact in groups? Consider the discussion above about the effects of fear as analyzed through the Physics of Success and observable in the Improvement Engine. The Physics traced to the following effects:

1) Heightening the likelihood of wrong choices
2) Shortening the organizational horizon

3) Reducing productivity—or at least diverting productivity toward unaligned objectives.

The Engine pointed out these further effects:

1) Decrease in levels of trust
2) Lengthening of cycle times for decision making and, therefore, improvement
3) Interference with aligned learning

Let's consider for a moment the effect of anger through the lens of one other model—The Ladder of Inference. Anger places you at the top of the Ladder of Inference, acting not on sound judgment from observation, but on emotional reactions to perceived threats. The reaction of the person you are dealing with, whether angry or afraid, is usually to stand there as well. You can see it in their eyes. This is a highly unpredictable and therefore volatile situation. Volatility—lack of predictability—is not trustworthy; the Engine tells us that the effects will thus soon lead to problems. You simply cannot know what eventual consequences the imposition of fear will bring. It might bring you compliance, but even in a compliant mode, people are usually resisting in at least a passive, if not, in fact, a very active way (see references to slave labor issues below.) It can backfire entirely and bring on rebellion. The consequences of kindness, however, are much more predictable and—I hope you will agree—more predictably beneficial.

There is an interesting exercise you may take on that I discovered quite by accident while researching this book. In trying to find examples of slave labor resistance, especially from World War II prison camps, I entered the words "labor" and "sabotage" in an Internet search engine. The results surprised me; they might surprise you as well. I found thousands of hits, but few having to do with the topic I had in mind. Instead, most of the references were to sabotage in the course of various labor vs. management conflicts in modern times. Let me make clear that I do not in any way sympathize with the destruction of property (and the usually overlooked risk of human life and limb) that most of these references described; neither the perceived offenses nor the ends justify such behavior, in my opinion. However, I could not help but notice that these stories certainly reflected on the volatility of fear. When people's livelihoods are perceived to be threatened, their behavior becomes increasingly unpredictable.

As a function of leadership, motivation should involve giving people reasons to do what the organization wants them to do, or at least those things which, in the individual's perspective, are in alignment with the organization's purpose. The effects shown above would indicate that anger works counter to this objective. Why, then, would we consider anger as a motivational tool?

The answer is mostly linked with either impatience or the perception of control. Anger—and therefore fear—is actually a pretty good motivator in the short term, and its powerful immediate effect gives us the belief that it is a good tool for quickly establishing control of a situation. We have already shown, however, that fear reduces an organization's horizon. Fear is mostly a temporary motivator—it arises to meet threatening circumstances. People driven by fear are therefore more temporarily motivated and tend to look only at that which is threatening in their immediate surroundings. Fear will cause them to see less and less of the horizon and less and less of the "big picture." As a motivator, then, it lacks permanence and stability. In graphic form, the effects of an environment of fear vs. an environment of trust, as they both relate to increasing performance over time, would look like this:

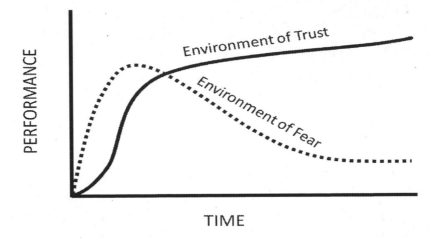

In the early going, fear will get people moving quickly. Over time, however, they will become conditioned to the fear (unless fear is continually revived—see the graph on "Effort" below), and performance will degrade as people put more of their Engine to work on self-preservation. Trust might get started a little slower, as you take time to build understanding. After that, however, performance will continue to increase—obviously a better long-term scenario.

Impatience is an interesting factor to consider in all this, especially as it relates to a perception of control. I am sure most of you can recall a person in a position of power who quite evidently wanted to have immediate control of every situation. This person is practically a stereotype, after all. Such people, from top-down bosses all the way up to dictators, enjoy the illusion of control because they get instant gratification when commands are carried out. The illusory nature of control for a dictator comes from the fact that what the organization *actually* learns—and daily improves—is the ability to maintain a mask of compliance and conformance. (A delightful example of this came from a conference I attended in the early 1990's. In hallway conversation with some consultants, I heard a story from one about an Eastern European shoe manufacturer. Before the Berlin Wall came down, this company had responded solely to instructions from the government about how much to produce. One day, they got instructions to double their output—with no allowance for more resources to do so. Knowing objections were pointless, they racked their brains to come up with a solution. It was finally found in the way their production was measured: boxes of shoes. They immediately started putting one shoe in each box. Most interestingly, this story shows a broken organizational Engine as far as the government goes, but a creative, "out of the box"—pun intended—Engine for the manufacturer.)

Those who pursue motivation through fear must also continually renew and reinvent their application of it, as people become numb to fear or eventually transform fear to anger and/or resistance. Leaders, people who "teach people to fish," can move on to other things knowing that the followers will continue aligned work because it meets their intrinsic needs. The dictator maintains power by controlling fish distribution— but he is then trapped in the task of providing fish. The graph below shows how effort required to sustain performance in a fear-based environment compares to effort required in a trust-based environment:

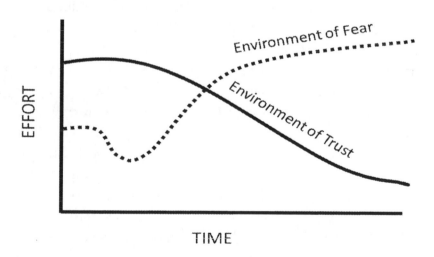

Again, the early going seems to favor fear. A small amount of effort here (it doesn't take much of the right kind of effort to scare people) can bring quick compliance. If the fear is substantial, even less effort will be required in the near term. In the long term, however, as people desensitize to the fear, new applications of different kinds of fear will be required. If the fear is built on dependence, maintaining that dependence will also require effort. Trust wins again in the long term. Motivated and (more or less) fearless, people in a trust-based environment need little more than direction.

A final point about anger as a motivator—anger expressed toward issues or external threats may be useful. It is not directed at the organization's members, so it has little of the risks described above. Like the appropriate type of parental anger, it may—if used at an appropriate level of control—instill an equally appropriate level of caution and competitiveness. There has been some debate about the value of competition, but I would offer the following personal observation: Competition as a motivator can actually be great. The problem comes when competition is interpersonal in arenas where trust is required between those persons. Compare—within the rules— against a clock or a standard or an external competitor—great, I say! This is the difference between the sports variety of competition and the professional variety practiced within organizations—the professional variety is quite obviously based on more arbitrary standards (witness the number of poor performers in high positions) and the methods are more questionable (there are no umpires—only authority). This makes all of those sports/business analogies questionable, in my opinion. In sports, we do not much admire a "victory at all costs" approach if that cost includes cheating, or if people win despite obviously inferior performance. Recent national news (Enron) as well as most people's personal experience show that organizations too often reward success achieved at the expense of ethics or good manners. Such success seems unlikely to be long-lived, as it does not survive scrutiny, and someone will inevitably call attention to it.

Fear and Success:

The above discussions should make it clear why fear and its counterpart, anger, should be less-than effective leadership tools. They are short-term tactics, not sustainable, long-term strategies. They take too much energy and repetition to sustain. What examples can we look to, though, to validate this thinking?

I will point to only a few. First of all, endless examples will not make the point any more effectively than the ones I have chosen, I think. Also, if you are not already convinced, you may find countless examples which might be used to refute me, for fear has been used frequently in the history of sad events on this planet to achieve obedience in the pursuit of accomplishments. I could, in turn, find an equal numbers of incidents where positive encouragement has worked wonders. I might argue that context is important in many of the situations where fear seems to be effective. You might then argue that I am merely dissembling. The fact is, if you are not already more than half convinced, you are unlikely to become more so. I have taken my best shots already. I include the following few illustrations more for the benefit of clarification than argument.

Consider first the history of empires. I mentioned context above, and this bit of thinking requires a lot of it. What we might consider a fear-based, dictatorial system today would not necessarily be viewed as such in an earlier historical context. The Roman Empire, for instance, would probably be regarded poorly in terms of today's human rights standards. Slavery, class distinctions, and the occasional conquering and subjugation of foreign peoples were common enough to horrify the New England Democrat and the Texas Republican alike. Even the worst of current governments would have been viewed as pretty standard fare in the context of medieval Europe. However, one thing seems consistently true about the history of fear as a governing strategy: When a government comes to be so ruthless as to be perceived unfair even in comparison to the current standard, that government tends to fall. At second glance, this seems rather logical—why should one be outraged at one's treatment unless, in comparison to some other tangible possibility, there is some significantly better scenario? If everybody gets the same treatment, even though that treatment be oppressive in the extreme, why should I bemoan my own repressed fortune?

The Improvement Engine explains why despotic empires inevitably collapse, despite occasional short-term success. Rule (leadership) through fear and intimidation ultimately chokes the Engine by "throttling" trust and respect. Such an empire is effectively hobbled in terms of its ability to improve. The entire system of such an empire, unable to improve itself, will either break of its own accord or be overcome by internal or external forces.

In retrospect, I believe this provides a relatively clear explanation for the unforeseen and, at the time, unimaginable, fall of the Berlin Wall. Two things were becoming apparent to leaders and followers alike behind that wall. First, the specter of a Western World just waiting to pounce on this outpost of Mother Russia was simply not a sustainable myth. I think that if I had been living in East Berlin in the 1980's, my thinking on that subject would have gone something like this: "Why should they want this mess over here? Look what they already have over there!" The Eastern Bloc was simply not as successful as the West, and by the 1980's, no amount of media censorship could keep that fact from anybody on the eastern side of that wall. It hadn't mattered whether the goals were inspiring; the Americans, for instance, had won the space race, despite a late start. It cannot have been lost on most citizens of the Soviet Union that their technology was simply lagging behind the West; they were imitators, not innovators. Blessedly, this is one instance of social pressure building to a critical head and finding release without catastrophic violence. The end of that chapter has yet to be written, but as long as media makes the images of the rest of the world available, it will be difficult for leaders to persuade—or intimidate—their people into continuing obedience if it is obvious that those leaders are not making their followers comparatively successful.

Perhaps an even better example of failure to prosper under a government devoted to control through fear is North Korea. I remember a picture which brought this point home in a stunningly clear way. It was a satellite photo of the entire Korean peninsula—taken at night. To the south of the border between South and North Korea, lights sparkled across the land. To the north, a few lights could be seen, mostly along the coast. The rest was dark; perhaps that is a metaphorical as well as a physical description. The North Korean government would surely respond that it fears nothing, and its people have no fear of the government. Why, then, does the government respond with such anger, and in such extreme language, to even the most mild provocations? The anger belies the inner fear. (Perhaps, in the West, we would do well to understand that they are afraid, not just prone to rages. It might make our words and actions toward them a lot more productive.) As for the people, if there is no fear between them and their government, then why is such tight control exercised over them? Why is isolation (a sure indicator of fear in itself) mandated? Why is dissent not allowed? I realize my own Western prejudices toward freedom of speech. Is it not apparent, though, that the nations which have allowed reasonably free expression of ideas have, in general, done better in providing a higher standard of living to their citizens than nations which have repressed such expression? Repression of the populace is an indicator of fear on the part of the leaders as well. It takes courage to face dissent. Repression is, frankly, a cowardly reaction to differing beliefs.

I spoke of inspirational goals; what could be a more compelling goal than Olympic gold? The people who pursue success in those arenas are already internally driven. If fear could add the last bit of motivation needed to bring an athlete to the podium, then wouldn't you think that Iraqi Olympic athletes from the Saddam Hussein era, who were tortured both as inspiration to victory and as punishment for defeat, would have made a better showing?

I have one final—and extreme—example to put before you. Surely, if you think that intimidation is the most effective means of gaining compliance, then a brief look at the stories of sabotage and resistance in the slave labor camps of both the Germans and the Japanese during World War II should be a final dissuader. Nowhere in history has there been such a well-documented attempt at building organizations governed by fear. The fear was absolute; death was perhaps the least of punishments handed out almost as a whim in these environments. The control was (or at least seems it should have been) equally absolute. If fear could have been successful, it should have worked here. From each of these environments, however, come the stories of resistance: sabotage of munitions in German factories, delays in construction in Japanese projects using P.O.W.'s. Fear gave the captors a high level of control, but that did not lead to a high level of performance.

Fear and Morality:

Whatever your opinions on religion, I think it can be generally agreed that what we usually view as the second half of the Ten Commandments correspond with our most basic agreed-upon views of what is acceptable in the treatment of other people: 1) Don't kill them, 2) Don't steal from them, 3) Don't tell damaging lies about—or to—them, 4) Don't have sex with their wives or husbands, and 5) Don't lust after the things that belong to them, as that will surely get you to the point of believing that one of the previous four is somehow justified. These are the basis for most of our laws and what we generally regard as "morality."

These are also the means of intimidation. Each of them leads to the possibility of creating fear and using it to influence—"motivate"—others. Threaten people with death or harm, and you may bend them to your will. Say that you will take the things they value most from them, and they will perhaps be inclined to do your bidding.

Intimidation and disrespect go hand in hand; using the former demonstrates the latter. Not only that, but using fear as a management tool reflects the lack of confidence leaders have in their followers; it demonstrates their own fear of not being able to motivate in an appropriate manner.

It's just wrong. Given the systemic effects I have shown about the issue, I rather feel that I shouldn't have to say more about it at this point.

Conclusion:

I started this chapter with a quote from Marie Curie: "Now is the time to understand more, that we may fear less." I confess I removed a bit of context from that quote. The sentence before that one goes like this: "Nothing in life is to be feared, it is only to be understood." I left that off because I simply don't agree with it. There are plenty of things in life that should be feared, at least if you use my definition of fear, which is simply to acknowledge that something is a threat. I think, honestly, my difference with Madame Curie is primarily in semantics. I think she is talking about the reaction to fear that I call terror—the view of perceived consequences from a threat (real or imagined makes little difference) that leads us to hopelessness, desperation, and irrational thinking and actions.

Fear, in the sense of perceiving and acknowledging real threats, is valuable and necessary to us. Our reactions to fear create problems, as does our tendency to perceive or exaggerate threats where little or no threat exists. Trying to use this witches' brew of conflicting motivations as a management tool is short-sighted, inefficient, potentially dangerous, and morally weak. It's a terrible waste of a good Engine.

Reflection:

- There is probably a lot to reflect on here, but I think the answers lie in a few simple questions:

  - Does your organization use intimidation as a management tool/ tactic in the workplace? Do you?
  - In your organization, does power make it impossible to object to bad behavior?
  - What are the long-term consequences of using fear to motivate short-term accomplishments? Is it really ever effective, or does it just feel good?

Chapter 8

Metrics Are Motives
(Measurement Drives Behavior)

"There is a measure in everything. There are fixed limits beyond which and short of which right cannot find a resting place."

Horace

"Measure not the work until the day's out and the labor done."

Elizabeth Barrett Browning

This will be a rather short chapter, but I would caution you in advance; do not equate briefness with unimportance. In fact, this chapter will advance concepts that should be foremost in your mind as you make what may be the most important decisions about your organization. What you measure—and how you react to those measurements—will probably do more than anything else to define the character and culture, and therefore, ultimately, the performance of your organization.

We all want to be successful, as most of us assume some level of happiness and comfort will attend that success. Each of us has a separate vision of success, and each is unique. Those unique visions are different definitions of success, and they may vary greatly from person to person, organization to organization, and culture to culture, even to the extent of creating conflict—even war. Quite naturally—in fact, often without even being conscious of it—we judge ourselves according to these standards. Our judgment of others is often based on our own definition of success as well, even when those people clearly articulate that theirs is a different vision than ours.

What is not often understood about these standards is that they form a system of measurements. Each aspect of success is evaluated by ourselves—and others—as a means to determine our level of success. That evaluation requires that we understand many of the basic elements of a measurement system. Not only must we understand what we are measuring, but we must also have at least some vague concepts of targets, for these are inherent in our vision. We also tend to have limits on these measures, so that we understand whether our current level of success is unacceptably low or (less common) beyond our ability to manage. Each definition of success thus becomes the basis of a sophisticated measurement system, allowing us to evaluate and compare our current realities and future prospects to our visions of success, usually across a rather broad set of metrics. That evaluation and comparison then informs our choices of future actions; we tend to (hopefully) reject potential actions that might generate results which are antithetical to our definition.

People have a relationship with data. In fact, we *need* data both to validate our beliefs and help us generate new ideas. Measurement—and analysis of the resulting data—is the mechanism of the people/data relationship. If there is anything the Improvement Engine does, it makes clear the nature of that relationship. I do not think it an exaggeration to say that the Engine models and defines the interaction between people and data, and that the interaction is based on—sometimes even defined by—trust.

Consider the complexity of the system. Start with the senses; each of them is a measurement device for phenomena around us. Vision processes light and images. Hearing processes sound. Touch, smell, and taste each have their measurement functions, which are used to answer questions like "Does this feel good?" or "What does that smell like?" The inputs from our senses are our data collection mechanism, looking at events and information at the bottom of the Ladder of Inference. Those measurements and observations are passed on to the intellect, where the process of attaching meaning begins, and further measurement occurs as we compare the new input to our stored data and create assumptions and conclusions. As we get near the top of the Ladder, our beliefs come into play, and our conscience and reason must review decisions and actions to make sure that they will not violate our beliefs. Each of these levels—sensory, intellectual, and ethical—is a part of the hugely complex measurement system that is built into each of us.

Most of us pursue a generically common model of success and can easily understand the desires of others. Some definitions, however, may seem irrational. For me, for instance, the good opinion of family members is important. Success would be a disappointment to me if it shamed my family. I have, however, known people who actively seek the opposite, and even seem to revel in their accomplishments in this vein. Such scenarios, and others where people pursue what seem like destructive or counterproductive ends, may seem sad or even tragic to most of us, but that judgment does nothing to alter the fact that there is still a system of measurement in place. I would say that at least one aspect of insanity involves malfunctioning or unbalanced measurement systems. The dysfunctional mind, from a Ladder of Inference perspective, attaches incorrect or disproportionate meaning to the events around it, and the consequently distorted decisions and actions coming off the top of the Ladder thus become irrational from the viewpoint of the observer. Note that the measurement system does not stop working in this case; it simply malfunctions. None of us ever really stops this measuring and judging. Somewhere in the back of our mind—in some cases people might call it our conscience—we must look at everything that happens to us and everything we might do to understand if there is alignment to our beliefs, and one of those beliefs (excepting the dysfunctional mind) is that we deserve the success we envision.

In groups, we establish more measurement systems, which define further standards and measures of success. In organizations, those systems often become formal and data-driven. Conversely, in varying cultures and societies, these measurement systems may be only tacitly understood and highly subjective. Many of us internalize these systems, or at least portions of them; when we do, standards by which others measure us become standards that we adopt as our own.

Conflicting measurement systems—especially between organizations and certainly between individuals—will reduce trust, as they will make motives suspect. Many Native Americans, for instance, used to consider taking an enemy's horse to be an act of bravery that advanced the warrior's status. Western culture, especially as it applies to this particular deed, regards such behavior as an act of simple thievery deserving a shameful death, usually by hanging. It is small wonder that the two parties found themselves at odds on this and other similar issues. Deeply religious cultures are certain to conflict with highly secular cultures. Militaristic societies will invariably find reasons to distrust—and, therefore, attempt to conquer—pacifist societies. Part of the problem here has to do with motives. Remember, we tend to measure others against our own standards; this means that when we try to understand the actions of others, we usually ascribe motives to those actions that would naturally follow from our own view. We do this in spite of the fact that it is close to impossible, unless one is equipped with a fertile imagination and/or a period of inquiring acquaintance, to fully and correctly interpret why anybody does anything. We simply don't understand their motives. How can you possibly trust what you do not understand? If you doubt the emotional impact of these misunderstandings, I would ask that you reflect on arguments you have had. Has anyone, during the course of such an argument, ever started an accusing sentence with something like, "You just want to . . .", and then proceeded to supply a motive for your previous words or actions that is completely unjust, unfair, and inaccurate? Makes you mad, doesn't it? (Of course, it can be equally maddening when they're right and it doesn't reflect well on you . . .) Our motives, since they stem from our beliefs, are a bit sacred to us, and so we are easily brought to a highly defensive state when they are impugned and/or misinterpreted.

Before we move on, take some time to evaluate this in your own experience. Where can you find evidence of this effect? Think about times when any of the following have happened to you:

- You found yourself in disagreement with another (or others) about priorities in a given situation.
- You found yourself at a loss to explain another person's behavior.
- You were misinterpreted or misunderstood.
- You misinterpreted or misunderstood someone else.
- You found yourself in disagreement with another's point of view about current events or the actions of people in the news.

In light of the above discussion, how many of those incidents were traceable to different sensibilities about how people and events should be measured? When were the actual measurements different? When were the targets and perceived acceptable limits of those measurements the cause of confusion or disagreement? How did this affect your interactions, especially your trust of others involved in the situation?

Measurement is not the full story here, however. Just as decisions are rather irrelevant unless accompanied by action, measurement is rather irrelevant unless you also consider the reaction to measurement. The real, underlying reason for measuring in the first place is to help us understand when to <u>do</u> something about a situation. At some point, limits are exceeded, and you are driven to take action to correct the situation (if a negative limit has been exceeded) or investigate the situation as an opportunity (if a positive limit has been exceeded).

I mentioned earlier that in organizations, measurement systems can become quite formal and structured, in which case they are reflected in policy and procedure. Suppose that you are in an organization where attendance is closely measured, but nothing ever happens to those who are frequently absent. What message do you think that sends, and what behaviors do you think are likely to ensue? Reaction to measurement is how measurements gain meaning. In the above situation, since there is no real reaction to the measurement, the attendance data are meaningless. Suppose you are in an organization that says it values the creativity of its members, but when you make suggestions, they are routinely either ignored or discounted. The reaction of the organization makes clear the real meaning of the measurement, doesn't it? A factor at work here is that in almost every organizational measurement system, and in many personal and cultural systems as well, there are, in fact, two systems, one explicit and the other implicit. The explicit system is one that is stated fairly clearly. In organizations, the explicit system can usually be found in documentation. The implicit system, however, is shown by our *reaction* to measurement. Sometimes the implicit system and the explicit system are a match; the reactions to measurement reinforce the stated system. The explicit system, however, may be somewhat of a sham, as in the case of the attendance data above. The news is not short on people who have made themselves famous, wealthy, or powerful while professing one set of beliefs, only to be discovered as having grievously violated exactly those beliefs. The downfalls of government and religious figures in such situations are sufficient evidence that the stated, explicit system of measurement may not be the one that actually drives reaction. At the end of the day, it is the implicit system that really matters, and that system is clearly observable through the organization's reactions to measurements. If the explicit system is a sham, people will quickly figure that out as they observe reactions.

Here we have come to the crux of the matter, as stated in the title of this chapter. Metrics are motives, and they drive our behavior. Our first loyalty is to our internal measurement system, as we seek first to satisfy the needs and desires that we believe will bring us some measure of security and contentment. Above this, we respond in a variety of ways to a multitude of organizational and cultural systems. We may internalize those systems and make them, essentially, part of our own. We may conform outwardly to these systems, even if we have not completely adopted them as our own, so that we will not be judged by others as being ideologically "out of step." We may even rebel against them if they chafe sufficiently against our internal system. Make no mistake, however; whether in compliance or rebellion, we are reacting to the measurement systems around us.

Let's look at a simple example. Imagine, for instance, that you are in the business of selling personal computers. Suppose that you want to promote sales of a super-duper, whiz-bang video card for the computer that will optimize the computer's performance in displaying graphics and video files. Such a card is most appropriate for people who have unusually high expectations for video performance, especially those who play graphic-intensive video games. Now suppose that, in order to promote sales of this card, you offer a bonus to your sales force of fifty dollars for each such card sold. Will some (most?) of your sales force try to sell that card to people who really do not need it and who may never benefit from it? Of course they will. Such a response will be aligned not only with their personal measurement system but with the organizational system as well.

Economists refer to this as "incentives"—providing rewards for performance and behavior that one wishes to encourage. Governments provide tax incentives to companies that act to promote government policies. Companies offer incentives to employees to promote behavior that advances the company toward its goals. Parents reward children for good behavior and punish them for bad behavior. (Incentives can be negative as well as positive.) A key concept taught in continuous improvement methodologies such as Six Sigma is the balancing of measures—making sure that focus on one metric does not damage another. Focusing too much on quantity of work may result in a drop in quality. Too much emphasis on quality may increase cost and cycle time. Improving one metric may result in the worsening of another.

For a glimpse of how contradictions in explicit vs. implicit systems can affect people, let me tell you about "Ron." "Ron" called me one night; he was a nodding social acquaintance more known to some friends than to me, but we had met. He had worked at the same company for several years, and he had learned early in his time there that taking more than about two days off at a time was bad for your future. It wasn't ever really discussed, but you knew it if you worked there. The mission was always critical, resources never sufficient; the company couldn't afford people to be away for long, etc. Then his Human Relations group started a series of "Work/Life Balance" classes. (Can you see it coming?) He attended. He listened, especially about the need for balancing time with family versus work. He took it to heart and, based on this new understanding of the explicit system, submitted a 1-week vacation request. And here the implicit system kicked in. The request was received with shock and dismay, along with inferences that this was really "letting the team down." He had gotten rather annoyed with this inconsistency between word and action, though, so he persisted, and the request was eventually, grudgingly, approved. When he returned, he was frequently reminded of the "favor" he had been granted. This lasted for weeks and might have gone on for months except for the marvelously ironic reason for his call. He needed no help with lofty improvement philosophies. He had heard from my friends that I used to teach Business Writing classes, and he wanted help from me in updating his resume. The words "deceived" and "betrayed" were both used in the conversation.

Now consider a more subtle example. I once worked with a company where a stated policy during the annual performance review cycle (involving, we would hope, some aspect of measurement) was to identify—and terminate—the lowest-performing five per cent of employees. The stated reasons (explicit system) for this had some surface logic; if you keep removing the bottom performers, you will be left with an organization of top performers. The organization, it was said, should look on this as accountability on the part of management to build the organization's performance. This should be seen as a good thing. Conversations with folks at the mid-management level were curious on this policy. Most would outwardly defend the system. There was, however, little enthusiasm in their defense. Essentially, they said it was a necessary but painful process, rather like abrading the skin from burn victims (one of their analogies, not mine). What was most curious, however, was their denial of the impact on the organization (the implicit system). They claimed the purpose was not to create fear but to set accountability for performance. As the review cycle approached, however, I could not help but notice the symptoms of a pervasive organizational fear. Communication and sharing of information decreased. Finger-pointing increased. Departments "ambushed" each other with accusations of poor support, execution, or follow-through. Individuals complained more about the perceived deficiencies of their associates. Verbal conflict increased. People's posture actually changed; heads hung lower, and eyes met less frequently when people passed each other in the halls. Whatever the stated purpose of the policy, its actual effect was fear, and management seemed diligent in ignoring the effects of that.

With the mention of fear, it seems appropriate to refer to the Improvement Engine to evaluate the impact of measurement systems on the cycle of improvement, specifically as it impacts trust. The video card sales example above represents a clash of measurement systems that will impact trust. In fact, every sales situation in the world has a basic, built-in trust barrier, as every sales situation represents a conflict of measurement systems between the salesperson and the customer. The salesperson seeks to maximize margin on the sale, in keeping with his or her personal benefits and the benefits of the company. The customer, of course, seeks exactly the opposite. A successful sale is, ultimately, the victory of trust over innate suspicion. When the customer trusts that he or she is getting the desired result at a fair/best price, the sale is made. The salesperson's job, therefore, is to win the trust of the customer. All of this is accomplished through a two-way learning system: the customer "teaches" the salesperson the requirements, while the salesperson "teaches" the customer about the superior benefits of the product or service. The Engine is at work again.

As I said it would be, this has been a short chapter, but the points to be made have been fairly simple, I think.

1) We all have a complex measurement system working within us.
2) Our measurements and standards—and those of others—drive our behavior.
3) When systems differ or conflict, lack of trust is likely to ensue.
4) As organizations, our choices of what to measure and our reactions to those measures should be a matter of the most intense consideration, for they are probably the most influential decisions in defining motivation, culture, and performance.

Reflection:

As the chapter was brief, so are the questions you should consider.

- What measures/standards (both conscious and subconscious) do you apply to the world and people around you? Are they appropriate and pertinent in that context?
- How do you react to what you measure? Is that reaction consistent with your stated measurement system? (Are there differences between your explicit and implicit measurement systems?)
- What behavior do you expect as a result of what you measure and how you react?
- Does your measurement system—including the performance review process—give people a clear picture of their individual performance as well as the group's?
- How does your measurement system impact trust between parties involved in events and processes around you?

Chapter 9

What to Do (Part 2)—Plus Tools!

> *"The only way to make a man trustworthy is to trust him."*
>
> **Henry Stimson**

In Chapter 5 I took a pause to translate theory into action. At the time, the Improvement Engine was incomplete, but as a learning model it had much to say to us. Since then, we have added one important concept to that model, which truly transformed it into the Improvement Engine. That concept was the entirely human element of trust. It may have seemed a simple addition, but it has complicated matters greatly. (I like to think of this as just creating more opportunity.) Trust and fear figure greatly in the working of the Engine, so it seems appropriate that we look at what our new knowledge tells us to do.

We will need to look at new issues raised by introducing trust to the Engine, but we should also review the actions already recommended to see what impact issues of trust may have. Here, in short list form, are the primary actions I recommended to you in Chapter 5:

- *Take an aggressive stance toward change.*
- *Change your perspective about what you think of as "communication"—it may be unidentified learning.*
- *Become an expert at identifying your own and your organization's soft spots.*

- *Understand learning—in the broad definition of this model—as a critical factor in the cycle time of improvement. Adjust your expectations accordingly.*
- *Don't use a "course catalog" approach to training. Design appropriate learning strategies for each specific need.*
- *Keep a critical eye on the flow of new and theoretical knowledge.*
- *Ensure appropriate preparation for training and follow-up after training.*
- *Examine processes, projects, and strategies for information hand-offs—identify them as separate learning actions, and use this model to plan them.*
- *Conduct "pre-learning" exercises before major projects.*
- *Learn how to state a proper learning objective. Review project plans for required behavior changes. Define them as learning objectives, and design appropriate learning for each such change. Focus at least as much on decision making as activity; correct execution depends first on correct decisions.*
- *Develop structured processes to learn from experience— especially bad experience.*
- *Examine relationships with suppliers and customers—and even across groups within your own organization—for possible learning opportunities—especially free ones!*

Before you listen to my take on all this, take a moment to develop your own insights. Which of these actions will affect trust? Which will be affected by trust? Review this list, put the Improvement Engine diagram in a visible spot, and do some thinking. Look for specific actions, but also think about larger themes at work here. I'll be here when you're ready . . .

All right, what did you find? How does an organization's ability to learn—and therefore to develop, and therefore to improve—react to issues of trust? Can you think of incidents where lack of trust affected your own ability to learn? Your organization's? Can you also recall incidents where sound relationships and organizational principles contributed to your own or your organization's learning?

I see two basic themes in the consideration of these issues.

First, the execution of successful learning is highly dependent on several factors around trust. The execution of training is a great process to look at in order to understand this. We should be able to trust that leaders pick the right thing for their organizations to learn. We should be able to trust that when we are sent to training, that training has been selected in order to improve our performance. We should be able to trust that such decisions were made carefully, based on our abilities, the organization's needs, and our own lack of skills (discussion of this last point has trust issues, as I have discussed). We should be able to trust that attention will be paid to the delivery of the training. Perhaps most importantly, we should be able to trust that we will have immediate opportunity to test our new skills and apply them. Most of the organizations I have observed do less than adequate work here. When we send people to learn something without understanding why, and when we fail to treat the training itself as a critical event, and when we fail to ensure application, we are insulting the people involved. Learning is the sole method the organization has to improve its people. If our execution of learning reflects lack of attention, lack of patience, lack of planning, and lack of commitment, all of that translates into a lack of respect for the learner. People tend to see the connection and respond appropriately.

Second, the organization's ability to see what it must learn is trust-dependent. As I have stated before, identifying learning needs means identifying the things you are not good at—yet. In an organization where blame and fear are operative, this is difficult to do in any productive manner. Also, do not forget that when it comes to new ideas, fear either stifles or misaligns creativity, so new information has a harder road to travel. A key component here is showing that the organization values its own wisdom and actively seeks that wisdom when confronting new challenges.

We are on the cusp of one of this book's biggest points. Since developing the Engine, I have frequently asked people a fascinating question: "*Why* do the methods and tools of continuous improvement work?" For most, especially those who dabble in my field, the question is a bit of a shock. They are used to being asked *how* continuous improvement works, not why. It makes a good exercise for a classic continuous improvement tool: 5 Why's. Ask yourself why continuous improvement works (you may substitute your favorite particular strategy, e.g., Six Sigma, if you wish). Whatever answer you get, ask "why?" again (pretend you're three years old again). Repeat that until you think you have the real answer. Do this now, before you read my answer below.

Here's my version:

Q: Why does continuous improvement work?
A: It forces thorough work and transparent/traceable decision making.

Q: Why are thorough work and transparent/traceable decision making important?
A: They provide proof that we are doing the right thing in the right way.

Q: Why is it important to prove those things?
A1: So people will trust that using the process will bring them success.
A2: So people will trust the conclusions and therefore respond favorably to required changes.

Trust in the process. Trust in the results. These are the reasons for the success of continuous improvement tools and methodologies.

Think about the implications of that.

One of the primary objectives of every improvement project should be to *generate trust*. The team members should trust the leader to use objective methods for analyzing causes and generating/selecting solutions. Sponsors should trust that they will be shown data that convincingly proves a successful approach and outcome. Stakeholders should trust that changes will be well-justified and not come as a surprise.

Why is this such an important point? Because we frequently confuse the abilities required to successfully implement improvement. Much attention is paid these days to the Six Sigma "Black Belt" set of capabilities, and those with the capabilities are much sought after to guide improvement. That set of capabilities, however, is focused on use of tools and statistics. It gives people the opportunity and the means to generate trust, but it does not focus on trust itself. As a result, the process is often seen, especially by the uninitiated, as one that is somewhat sterile, governed by rules, often impractical or trivial. Successful, significant improvement almost always involves changing people as well as things. A Black Belt ensures good data analysis and methodical approaches to decisions; it does not guarantee good leadership.

There is one other point that I believe deserves some discussion from Chapter 5. This is in regard to generating an organizational culture where sharing of knowledge is an acknowledged value. I have encountered many in my day who feel that teaching others is not only not part of their job, it is something that violates their own personal job security. Obviously, an underlying assumption to this thinking is that the organization will not value that person's wisdom as much if it is "distributed." Certainly, I have seen organizations where such fear is justified. However, the most effective organizations I have seen have not only encouraged but required that their best members teach, coach, and/or mentor others. I will have more to say on this in the chapter on what to do as a leader.

Now let us begin the discussion of new developments in the Engine as a result of adding the trust factor. Here are actions and approaches that will allow you to truly maximize the performance of your Engine.

- *   **Develop a culture of trust.**

All right, this isn't easy. It's also not impossible. It is *critical* to remember that, as I have said before, the Engine is not a "one knob" machine. You seek optimal, not simply maximized, levels of trust. The reasons for doing this should be amply justified by now. The question is how. First of all, let me recommend that you focus your efforts on the center box of the Improvement Engine. This is where the biggest obstacles to trust are usually created, as it is here where decisions are made.

Remember that trust for trust's sake is rather irrelevant. Personal trust does not always translate into organizational trust. Trust must be built around the communication and processing of important information. Meaningful communication is a two-way process, after all, and that should mean involving people in discussion of and decisions surrounding issues of some real importance.

Ultimately, there is no surer way to develop trust than to give it (note the quote which starts this chapter). However, unconditional trust is, frankly, foolhardy. In the words of Winston Churchill, "Trust—but verify." Follow up on commitments made to be sure there was satisfaction. The people whom I most trust meet one common description: they do what they say they will do.

There are some specific actions you can take to build trust:

-   Especially if groups are new to each other, or have a history of issues, and especially if they are expected to work together in an organizationally critical situation, have them identify small commitments (short term) that they can make to build trust. Assure and emphasize successful completion of early milestones. As people see others meeting commitments, they will not only gain trust in those individuals, they will be motivated to return the favor.

- Establish a few important ground rules for respectful, trustworthy behavior in your organization, and treat them as something close to sacred. Be careful not to go overboard here. Too many rules will invariably lead to trivialization. Try to make it a list of six or less.

- Read—and pay attention to—the recommendations of Dr. Stephen M. R. Covey in his book <u>The Speed of Trust</u>. He defines a structure for trust and 13 specific behaviors you can use to build trust. He also talks about making that trust scalable, from interpersonal to inter-organizational, to market, and ultimately to society at large. He discusses the practical boundaries of trust, and he even addresses ways to repair trust that is damaged.

- Be a role model. Even if all is chaos around you, be the person people can rely on for truth and commitment. Really.

- *Review your measurement system and ensure its alignment with organizational values.*

If your measurement system encourages untrustworthy behavior, or if it sets organizations against each other within the larger organization, nothing you do will help. Treat this as a top priority, and examine the issues thoroughly and frequently. The specifics of doing this will vary greatly from organization to organization, but here are some action guidelines.

- Create an organizational relationship diagram that shows how different groups depend on each other, then fill in the measurements that management most pays attention to for each group. Identify the conflicts. Change measurement systems where appropriate, or create trust-building communication processes between groups where conflict is inevitable (e.g., Finance says "save," Research and Development says "spend").

- Review carefully whether your measurements reflect your values—look for conflicts as well as omissions. Make sure your implicit and explicit measurement systems are aligned.

• ***Examine your meeting culture.***

A company's culture and its meetings are inextricable. It is in meetings that members learn what makes for successful behavior and image, because this is where people in lower parts of the organization get their best opportunity to see how leaders act outside of public speaking opportunities. Meetings mirror the values of the organizational culture. How people and ideas are treated there defines the culture. Many people think meetings are a waste of time. Many are. Follow the guidelines below to turn your meetings into occasions people will look forward to, as they know real results will be achieved from the time spent.

Here is an interesting question that may enlighten your next agenda: How are people expected to think or act differently as a result of that meeting? If you don't expect people to either think or behave differently after a meeting, then there is no reason for that meeting. How can you maximize their integration of information and their likelihood to act?

First of all, consider why meetings are held in your organization. There are basically two kinds of meetings: meetings where status is reviewed and meetings where decisions are made. The former are often ineffective; the latter count for everything. Status review is something that can generally be communicated in written form; it is simply a download of information. Certainly, status meetings allow for questions and information-sharing, but most of these meetings tend to be reviews of information that nobody is willing to synthesize and communicate beforehand in writing—easier to just have a meeting. I would point out that even these meetings can be turned to more productive ends if they focus on what people must actually learn from the information presented. I would also point out that the key "blind spot" in "status review"-type meetings is the assumption that "communication" is taking place. We must *learn* the current status—not just the facts of how much product sits in how many locations, not just how many customers are on the line at what time, but how those facts should affect our priorities, our actions, our decisions.

Meetings to make decisions tend to be more productive, but they tend to have problems with a phenomenon known in training circles as "circle yak-yak." This occurs when a topic is brought forward and one person after another discusses options, viewpoints, etc. Unless there is a visible process for collecting and processing the information put forward, people will inevitably repeat themselves, wander off-track, and generally make little progress on the issue. After about 45 minutes of this with no real progress, the group makes a decision out of desperation ("We only have this room for 15 more minutes!"), usually based on the most authoritative or loudest voice in the room. I'm sure you've all been in that meeting.

Continuous improvement tools are part of the answer to this; they ensure that information is collected and processed to arrive at a best—not desperate—solution. Basic meeting practices are also critical: having an agenda with a real purpose and timelines, sticking to that agenda, etc.

Many other behaviors from meetings reflect in the culture outside the meeting. Promptness, dependable attendance, action item completion—as they are handled in meetings, so they will be handled outside the meeting. Particularly, the way people treat each other in meetings will have an effect on the way they are treated elsewhere. If people learn that personal attacks, interruptions, or general disrespect are tolerated in meetings. especially by or from leaders, they will logically assume that these are the behaviors that management expects from its successful members.

So, what do you do about this?

- Ensure that the ground rules mentioned above are practiced religiously in meetings.

- Practice basic good meeting skills—use agendas and time limits, and be sure there is a real purpose for the meeting in the first place. Record—and follow up on—action items and decisions.

- Maximize information sharing before the meeting, so that meeting time can be focused on making decisions about that information.

- Use tools in meetings to collect and process input.

- Where status meetings are necessary, make sure there are structured opportunities to discuss how the information should affect future decisions and actions.

- Provide facilities in rooms that will make meetings more productive. Make sure flip charts and/or boards are available to record information and keep it visible. Invest in making meeting rooms places where good decisions can be made.

- Establish a culture of starting and ending meetings on time, with all necessary members—or empowered representatives—in attendance (leadership examples are critical here). Yes, this will improve your meeting productivity, but it will also help establish a culture of doing what you say you're going to do.

- ***Train decision making at least as much as activity.***

Action requires first that a decision to take action be made; before even that, there must be recognition of the need to make a decision. Training classes, in general, tend to focus on behavior changes and the actions that attend that change. This ensures that people understand the "what" and "how" of a new behavior—as I said in Chapter 5, how to "read the map." What is often left untrained, or at least given insufficient focus, are the "when" and the "why" (these only come with actually "knowing the territory"). This is not always a bad thing. Frankly, training classes are often not the best place to learn this; it may be better learned through coaching/mentoring in a real work situation. The key point here is that we do not simply wish to achieve correct behavior. If people do the right thing in the right way in the wrong situation, failure still attends the outcome. We want to ensure that the decision process that leads people to take action in the first place is correct. Behavior is a symptom; the decisions leading to that behavior are the root cause. If continuous improvement methodologies teach anything, it is that we should address root causes in order to fix issues permanently.

How does trust bear on this? Simple—people recognize when they are given authority and responsibility, and decisions are at the heart of both.

Here are some things you can do to influence this in your organization:

- Distinguish between "rules" and "principles"; the former are supposed to derive from the latter. Make sure that people understand the principles associated with their process and the organizational values. If they find that obeying the rules brings them in conflict with the principles, they should regard that as a major "red light" in regard either to their thinking or the rules themselves.

- Provide coaching and mentoring support to those who are making complex new decisions based on new learning. Training may have provided them with ability, but it is usually the organization which provides context.

- **Make everyone a teacher, everyone a learner.**

I made this point previously, but in the context of trust, it deserves another look and some definitive action recommendations. The key issue here is to make sure that organizational behavior at every level shows a respect for learning. There is no way I know to accomplish this more effectively than to involve everyone actively in the learning process.

Here are some things you should do about this (warning—you won't like the last one):

- Make it clear from the interview process forward that sharing of wisdom is a key value of the organization and an expectation of all members.

- Assign teaching—as well as learning to your people. They may gripe, but you must insist on the fact that they are all responsible for improving the organization, not just sustaining it—and improvement requires learning.

- Counsel, marginalize, and if necessary, terminate those who violate this value. (Sorry . . . I told you that you wouldn't like this one.)

- ### *Invest in trust.*

I was once discussing the Engine with a colleague who made a wonderful comment about the situation at hand. He said, "Trust is not in the budget." In a sense, he was right. It is certainly not purchasable as an outright commodity (what a fine dream, though . . .), and it looks a bit weak as a justification on a purchase request. The logic I have brought you through to get here, though, should help you see that some investment for that purpose is justified. Like anything else in the world, trust will cost you something. Make that investment, but make it wisely. As I have said, trust for trust's sake is not your goal. Make sure your financial investments in it are geared toward genuine organizational outcomes. Avoid "ropes course" types of training and other so-called team-building events unless there is a specific plan to immediately turn the results of such activities into mutual work on shared issues relative to the organization's needs. Use money to buy the things that enable trust and support good decision making, like adequately equipped classrooms and meeting rooms.

Only part of the investment required is financial, though. You must also invest emotionally, and you must invest time. Commit to trust. Teach trust. Earn trust. These are strategies that will cost you some investment of yourself, but the reward will be worth it when you see the positive changes in the speed and quality of decision making and the resulting improvement.

Specifically:

- Talk about trust. Make it one of the more highly discussed topics in your organization. Oddly enough, when you consider how much that word has affected this book, the word is not one I have frequently encountered in business situations. It is almost as though people avoid it as too personal, emotional or "soft." The word "trust" has an impact with people when you bring it up in the context of improvement. Maximize that value through frank and open discussions about how trust is affecting your organization's performance.

- Devote time to trust. I think you know what I mean here, and we don't do enough of it.

- Don't dismiss financial investments in trust. The previous chapters of this book provide all the justification you need.

• **Use the Engine to analyze, address, and repair trust issues.**

From my own personal use of the Engine, I can tell you that you want to post a copy of the Engine diagram in a visible place for frequent reference. It is a tool to be used, not just remembered. Spend some time staring at it and imagining how your processes—and the problems with them—map to the Engine. Focus on the trust and respect boxes, and consider how poor learning and communication (same thing!) are affecting issues there. As practice, make a list of the three best and three worst organizational experiences you've ever had, and practice pointing to the place on the Engine diagram where things went right or wrong. You'll be surprised how often the boxes on the right and left are not where the problem was caused. More frequently than you would think, you will find yourself pointing at some place in between those boxes, or at one of the trust/respect entries/exits to those boxes. In other words, the problem wasn't simply a bad idea or failure to execute the plan. The problem was a failure to make a good plan to implement the idea, or failing to treat people's need for information with the respect it deserves, or failing to enlist and establish relationships among stakeholders, customers, etc. In short, failing to develop trust or failing to understand vital aspects of communication/learning.

Most of this is just about actually *using* the Engine, so there isn't much to say about how that I haven't already said. Thus I recommend only one action based on this point"

- Don't let the Improvement Engine just sit in its book. Bring it out in the open where it can do some good. Post it in meeting rooms so that you can refer to it in groups and examine its lessons.

- ### *Learn to disagree without damaging trust.*

Disagreement can be an important positive force/catalyst for improvement, as long as you respect it and deliver feedback about it respectfully. Especially in creative situations (the Invent side of the Engine), disagreement can prompt new ideas, improvement of existing ideas, and, in general, a thorough examination of the situation at hand.

The entire problem with disagreement is its frequently negative emotional impact. Now remember the chapter on fear. The primary cause of hostile reactions is fear. If people are getting heated emotionally as a result of discussing ideas, it is because they feel threatened. In fact, conflicting ideas are not threats; they are opportunities. Most of the trick here is in getting emotions—particularly fear—out of the decision making process.

So how do you do that?

- Use continuous improvement tools to gather information about the conflict; they make the points of disagreement visible and objective. List pro's and con's. Look for places where the solutions are similar and different, and look for synergistic possibilities as a result of that thinking.

- Insist that disagreements be solved with data, not authority, politics, threats, or vocal volume. If you have the right viewpoint, you should be able to prove it, and that requires data.

• **_Use tools and structured processes for decision making._**

I've referenced this point a few times already, but it deserves emphasis. A *lot* of emphasis. This is a highly visible, actionable step that can be taken more or less immediately to improve decision speed and quality as well as trust in the process and results. Accordingly, I want to show you how to use several of them to speed decision making, improve decision quality, build trust, and/or lead to consensus—in other words, with an eye to the Improvement Engine. This will allow you to take that highly visible step forward quickly.

In general, these tools contribute to the above outcomes by:

- ensuring that all useful data—even very subjective data, if appropriate (e.g., brainstorming results)—is gathered to give a solid foundation to decision making
- providing a visible, step-by-step process for processing data
- creating a record of decisions that is useful in communicating to (teaching . . .) others and allows review and refinement of decisions
- . . . all of which I include in the term "Thorough, Transparent, and Traceable"

My instructions will be relatively brief; I will focus mostly on how they support concepts related to the Improvement Engine. If you need more detailed instructions on exactly how to use these—and many other— tools, there are web resources (look under "Six Sigma) or you may refer to the <u>Memory Jogger</u> series. There are many other tools than those I list below, but those below represent the core of what is taught in most

Six Sigma programs—the so-called "Yellow Belt" and "Green Belt" level tools. These tools are the foundation for such programs, the most essential of the tools, the equivalent of drills, screwdrivers, and saws to a carpenter. Here is a list of them:

- **Brainstorming**
- **Voting**
- **Problem Statement**
- **SIPOC**
- **Process Maps**
- **Trust Touch (My invention, not a part of the traditional Six Sigma tool kit)**
- **Summary Statistics and Charts**
- **Cause/Effect Diagram**
- **Decision Criteria Matrix**
- **Action Plan**
- **Force Field Analysis**
- **Cost/Benefit Analysis**

Let's just go through them one at a time, shall we?

- **Brainstorming**
  Purpose: Brainstorming, if conducted correctly, simply generates the most creativity/ideas from a group.

  How it Works: I have already discussed this process in some detail. Two key principles to correct execution:

  1) Have people write down all the ideas they can think of <u>before</u> there is any discussion of the topic except to clarify it.
  2) Collect and present ideas in a way that respects and expects everybody's complete participation; little if any discussion, <u>especially</u> not criticism.

Why it Works: This process ensures that participants' ideas will be treated with respect, and that all ideas will be presented for fair consideration.

Pitfalls: Violate either of the two key principles and you will reduce the amount and creativity of the ideas, which will ultimately reduce the quality of your decisions.

- **Voting**

   Purpose: Process large lists of ideas to reduce them to a few best.

   How it Works: There are many processes for voting. One that works for me most often is to give people a number of votes equal to the number of ideas divided by three (or so) up to a maximum of ten votes. Then have participants place their votes—only one vote per idea—on what they consider the best ideas. In the end, this gives a priority ranking to all the ideas in a quick and fair manner, as long as the judgment of the participants is informed and reliable. This multi-voting process is excellent for getting a large list down to a critical few that can then be examined in more detail, often using a Decision Criteria Matrix (see below).

   Why it Works: It's quick and generally perceived as fair.

   Pitfalls: 1) Not having the right people or not having those people well-informed. 2) Failing to ask, at the end, if some idea that did not "make the cut" needs further exploration. Perhaps its advantages were not clearly communicated.

- **Problem Statement**

   Purpose: Explain, at the beginning of an improvement effort, what you intend to accomplish and why.

   How it Works: The Problem Statement may have several elements; the following are key:

1) As-Is vs. Desired State—explains, with reference to data and circumstances, what the current conditions are and what the desired change will look like in the most measurable terms possible. This usually contains a goal with the following characteristics:

    a. The goal is specific; it tells exactly what will be accomplished.

    b. The goal is measurable; there is a number or condition to be reached that can be stated, and once supposedly achieved, proven.

    c. The goal is achievable—aggressive, hopefully, but not so huge as to wither a project team's confidence.

    d. The goal is relevant—it is aligned with the needs and directions of the organization and its customers.

    e. The goal I time-bounded—there is a specific date by which the improvement will be complete and validated.

2) Why Selected—explains why, in the midst of dozens or even hundreds of things you might choose to improve, you picked this one. Why is it a priority? How does it make life better for customers? How does it reduce cost or improve quality, and why is it important now, from a business perspective, to address this issue? Will costs decrease? Will revenue increase? Will you increase capability or capacity?

3) Scope—Answers the following questions:

    a. Where and how broad will be the impact?

    b. Who and what will be affected?

    Often an "Is/Is Not" approach is taken to this. This simply lists what will be affected (processes, products, organizations, equipment, regions, etc.) on one side and on the other lists any contrasting factors that will not be affected.

4) Stakeholder Analysis—shows what people, organizations, suppliers, or customers will be affected by this change. Also usually starts the process of identifying their concerns. Helps identify what people to involve, which to communicate with.

Why it Works: First of all, it says what you are going to do, the first step of commitment. Second, it shows you have done a <u>thorough</u> job of justifying your focus on this issue and the resources that may be required to improve it. Third, it makes your decision on this fundamental matter both <u>transparent</u> (it is clearly evident what you are doing) and <u>traceable</u> (it is equally evident why).

Pitfalls: People are usually reluctant to commit, especially in a business environment where consequences are high and/or highly visible. Make sure goals include the "measurable" and "time-bounded" elements. Without these, there is no commitment.

- **SIPOC**
  Purpose: List and establish process relationships between suppliers, their inputs to the process, the process they feed, the outputs of that process, and the customers who must use those outputs. (SIPOC stands for Supplier, Input, Process, Output, Customer.)

  How it Works: On the surface, it is pretty simple. Here is an example (NOT a good one, just a sample to show how it works—see comments about not using this tool thoroughly below):

S	I		P	O		C
Suppliers	Inputs		Process	Outputs		Customers
	Input	Req's		Output	Req's	
Customer	Order	Address Product	Enter Order	Internal Work Order	Order #	Assemblers
Supplier 1	Parts	5" Long 7" Wide	Build Product	Product	Pass QA	Customer

In each column, list all of the things you can think of. Consider inputs and outputs of all natures: products, decisions, materials, data, etc. Adding the "Requirements" column in the Input and Output columns may shed light on the concerns of stakeholders. This is a good tool for identifying stakeholders, potential team members, and issues they are likely to care about.

Why it Works: Identifies who needs to be "in the loop" for this effort. Getting the right people involved increases team confidence as well as capability. If rigorously examined, this tool can also provide clues about any trust issues likely to arise, as the concerns of stakeholders have been identified, and any potential threat to those concerns should be foreseeable.

Pitfalls: The biggest failure I see in using this tool is a lack of thoroughness. Too often, this tool is simply "pencil whipped"; only the obvious elements are identified. They look like the example above.

- **Process Maps**
  Purpose: Diagram the steps in a process for both communication and analysis purposes.

  How it Works: (Actually, I'm not going to tell you how to make one—a bit too complicated for this space. There are plenty of places to learn how to do process maps, however; I'd start with the Memory Jogger.) There are many formats for process flows, probably the most widespread being the Process Flow Map and the Value Stream Map. The former tend to be more detailed and include all of the decisions, reworks, exceptions, etc. in the process. They are generally best used to find where defects and excess variation (Six Sigma stuff) are affecting the process. The latter tends to be less detailed but contain more information on cycle time, inventory, etc. They are generally aimed at identifying waste and process points that do not work in a continuous flow (the Lean stuff).

Why it Works: This tool has two primary impacts from an Improvement Engine standpoint. First, it shows that you have taken time to accurately and completely understand the process—and therefore something about the world its stakeholders live in. Second, it speeds communication and discussion of opportunities in the process, as it is a visible, shareable tool.

Pitfalls: Make sure you document the process the way it is actually done—this can only be accomplished be observation. Written procedures are too often incomplete (especially with regard to exceptions) or downright inaccurate.

- **Trust Touch**
  Purpose: As I mentioned above, this is my own invention. It allows you to quantify, at least in an approximate way, the level of trust associated with any activity, input, output, or organizational/interpersonal interaction.

  How it Works: Use the indicating factors I listed earlier in the book to identify circumstances which are affecting trust levels. Assign that level a number from 1 to 5.

LOW TRUST	HIGH TRUST
1--5	
High Risk	Low Risk
Input(s)/Outputs Unreliable	Input(s)/Outputs Reliable
Process Not Capable	Process Capable
Many/High Level Signatures	No Signatures
Multiple, Rigorous Controls	No Controls
Win/Lose Expectation	Win/Win Expectation
Unilateral Concerns	Mutual Concerns
Communication on Need	Continuous Communication
Purpose/Goal Unclear	Purpose/Goal Clear
Method Unknown/Doubtful	Clear, Proven Method

On a SIPOC or any type of process map, place a "T" and a trust level number (e.g., "T4" for a trust level of 4) wherever there are interactions. This is a "Trust Touch"—a place where trust can affect process performance. How much do people trust their inputs? How about their own outputs? Are there differences in perceptions? All of these will be apparent and (admittedly with some subjectivity, which can be lessened by getting consensus on these trust levels from a group) quantifiable.

Why it Works: You are actually identifying the areas where trust will affect your process and your attempts to improve it.

Pitfalls: Remember that improvement as a result of this analysis is not simply a matter of maximizing trust, it is a matter of optimizing trust appropriately at each interaction point given real risks and opportunities.

• **Summary Statistics and Charts**
  Purpose: Statistics and charts allow for the quick and more complete communication of data and their potential meaning.

  How it Works: As with process maps, I will refrain from specific instructions. Summary statistics (range, average, standard deviation, correlation coefficient, etc.) condense large amounts of data down to one or a few numbers. The numbers often provide insights to data that simply aren't visible in scanning a spread sheet. Summary statistics inform and validate decisions. Charts reduce large amounts of data to a picture. The picture allows faster understanding of the data presented and gives visual clues for analysis.

Why it Works: These are simply better tools to teach people about what the data around them is saying. Taking the time to generate them shows you value this communication; you are preparing to teach the organization how to solve this problem. People will trust data more than most other things, subject to the pitfall mentioned below.

Pitfalls: Listen to statistics with absolute honesty. The connection between statistics and damn lies is well documented; don't be a participating victim.

- **Cause/Effect Diagram**
  Purpose: Create a thorough list of potential causes for an observed effect. Group those causes in major categories based on their source and identify relationships between causes (i.e., what are causes of the causes?).

  How it Works: The format for this tool is usually a "fishbone diagram": here is an example:

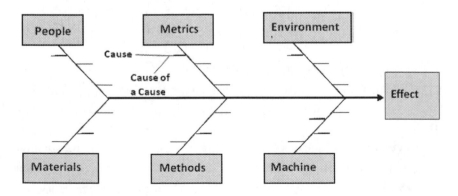

The "Effect" box contains either an undesirable or a desirable result observed in the current process or foreseeable in the future process. Brainstorming is the fastest way to populate the diagram with potential causes.

Why it Works: By maximizing the input with brainstorming, the Cause and Effect Diagram assures thorough consideration of all the things acting on the process. This reduces the likelihood of acting on preconceived ideas about how to fix or improve the process. Ranking methods (see the Memory Jogger for instructions) have been specifically tailored for this tool to consider both the frequency/likelihood of these causes having a major effect as well as the difficulty involved in making changes (impact vs. effort). Because it is a visible document, it makes communication and discussion easy and productive while providing a history of thinking and decision making (transparency and traceability). Finally, because this tool drives groups toward fixing causes instead of simply applying process "band-aids," it builds long-term faith, for this project and perhaps for the organization at large, that meaningful, sustainable improvement will be achieved.

Pitfalls: I have already discussed the danger of becoming too focused on the tool and its exactly correct use as opposed to the result expected from it. For some reason, this tool gets stuck in this circumstance a lot. I have already told you one story about a spectacular meltdown while using this tool; there are others, just less spectacular. Keep focused on the purpose of the tool—identifying causes you can address.

- **Decision Criteria Matrix**
  Purpose: Make a final choice from among a few proposed options or courses of action.

How it Works: I have already explained how this tool works in the story about "saving the meeting" that was supposed to last all afternoon as well as the story of Bob, who changed his mind as a result of this tool despite political expectations. Here is an example:

DECISION: WHAT SHOULD I DO WITH MY VACATION TIME?		Visit Family	Travel	Stay Home	Take it Later
MUST HAVES:					
Relaxation		Yes	Yes	Yes	No
OTHER CRITERIA:	PRI	FIT / PRI x FIT			
Recreation	1	2 / 2	3 / 3	1 / 1	N/A
Learning	2	2 / 4	3 / 6	1 / 2	N/A
Comfort	3	3 / 9	1 / 3	3 / 9	N/A
Get Things Done	3	1 / 3	1 / 3	3 / 9	N/A
Adventure	2	2 / 4	3 / 6	1 / 2	N/A
TOTALS:		22	21	23	N/A

Across the top of the Matrix are the potential solutions—in this case, alternative uses of vacation time. Down the left hand side of the Matrix are the criteria that should be applied in making the decision (recreation, learning, etc.). Not all of these criteria have the same priority. Some (in this case one: comfort) are "must haves": criteria that <u>must</u> be met for the decision to be considered successful. Alternatives which do not meet these criteria are eliminated from consideration (note that "take it later" does not meet this criterion, so it drops out of the running right there). The "other criteria" are those that have varying priorities and must be balanced against each other. This is managed in the "pri" (priority) column by assigning a numerical rating to each of the criteria. (Usually, a 1 to 3, as above, or 1 to 5 scale is used; the higher number indicates higher importance/priority.) Then each of the solutions that has passed the "must have" hurdle is judged for its "fit" to each criterion—how well it meets that desired purpose. That number is the first of the two in the "fit/pri x fit" column under each option. (The same scale for rating priorities is used to rate fit; the higher number indicates that solution will do well in meeting that criterion.) The second number in this column is the result of multiplying the "pri" number by the "fit" number. Finally, adding those numbers in each column gives you a total that indicates the "best" solution. (As I read this step by step, it sounds easier than it is. Mind you, it's a lot easier—and better—than the usual "circle yak-yak" alternative, but be sure to read the "Pitfalls" section on this one.)

Why it Works:—This tool simply provides a clear process for collecting, discussing, and coming to consensus upon a course of action amid all the concerns that course of action implies. If the process of determining options has been perceived as fair and objective, people will be in agreement with those already. The criteria are critical to trust. "Criteria" masks the real power of these factors; these are the things people care about! Using this tool acknowledges each concern and more or less forces consideration of that by all others involved in the decision. Widely varying perceptions on the "priority" numbers can reveal agendas—or valid, unconsidered points of view. Used correctly, it once again meets the "thorough, transparent, and traceable" requirements. As a document, it provides a record of exactly what influenced you to decide as you did. Really, now—wouldn't you have loved to see one of these attached to some organizational decisions you've experienced? If you've ever wondered, "Why, of all things, did they choose *that*?" then this would have at least answered. Imagine if politicians were required to attach one of these to each vote in Congress . . .

Pitfalls: As I said above, this tool sounds pretty easy. That may be a bit deceptive. The point is, you can't simply hammer through this. Each criterion, each rating number needs consensus—not majority, but consensus, meaning all can support it. This often requires high levels of facilitation skills. Several minutes spent talking about a simple priority number can feel like "bogging down" over trivia. Remember that taking time here speeds the final result.

- **Action Plan**

  Purpose: In various forms, from action item lists to Gantt or "milestone" charts, this tool does one basic thing; it tells you <u>who</u> is going to do <u>what</u> by <u>when</u>, sometimes including information on the length of time for the action.

  How it Works: Make a list of all the actions required to complete your purpose (brainstorming is a great tool here). For each action, assign a "champion" or person responsible for ensuring that this action is completed. Define a date by which each action will be completed. For more oversight, also identify when work on that action will begin.

  Why it Works: Brutally simple—you just said what you are going to do. In fact, you committed to it on paper. This is the first in the "say what you do, do what you say, prove it" triad. You have taken a firm step in establishing trust in your intentions. This tool gives confidence both to the team (that there is a visible path to success) and to sponsors and management (there is accountability, a concrete plan, and a commitment to depend on in making other decisions).

  Pitfalls: Just make sure you are thorough and get real agreement on the commitments made. Again, this is harder to do than to say. Obviously, this can be a very good way to be highly visible in any failures to estimate well. Make sure, especially in first attempts, to be a bit pessimistic about your schedule. I do not intend to teach project planning here, so I will simply say that there are—and I think it is fairly clear how and why—several potential pitfalls in trying to predict what can be done and commit to doing it. A large part of getting good at this is as simple as getting to Carnegie Hall: practice, practice, practice.

- **Force Field Analysis**

  Purpose: Identify the factors in the environment—including people—who will positively influence, or support, your intent. Identify factors as well which will resist you—for whatever reason. Assign some rating to the force each factor will apply. Use the result to define actions you may need to undertake in order to reduce resistance or increase the force pushing with you.

  How it Works: Let's just look at one:

Force Field Analysis – Release of Upgrade	
Driving Forces	**Restraining Forces**
ENVIRONMENT	ENVIRONMENT
Current complaints ➡️	⬅️ Time
Profit/Revenue ➡️	← Need Misunderstood
Competition ➡️	
	PEOPLE/GROUPS
PEOPLE/GROUPS ➡️	⬅️ Quality
V.P. of Sales	

  On the left side, list "driving forces"—the things working with you in your effort. On the right, list "restraining forces"—the things that may resist or downright oppose your effort. The arrows above indicate what level of force is applied by that factor; thicker arrows mean more force (you could easily use numbers or bars of varying length as well; the arrows are just traditional). In the example above, then, complaints about the current product version are driving this organization to release an upgrade— and that voice is quite loud, as shown by the thick arrow. The projected revenue/profit are motivators as well, but not as strong as the complaints. Quality will have to be convinced that the new product is reliable, and that will take some work. Time is a major factor; in this case, there is a narrow and imminent time window. By the way, the example above has two sections: "environment" and "people/groups." This is <u>not</u> traditional. I find this tool useful for identifying trust issues between individuals or groups; that is why I specifically look at them. BE CAREFUL with this; see Pitfalls.

Why it Works: This is a great tool for identifying actions that are not part of the "just get it done" path of thinking. In order for an effort to be successful, driving forces have to *win*. This just helps ensure thorough thinking about all the factors that may affect success. Using it specifically to identify trust issues between people and groups simply incorporates the ideas of the Improvement Engine, using a tool already familiar to many continuous improvement practitioners.

Pitfalls: First of all, this tool is useless unless it is used to identify actions you have not yet built into your plan. Second, if you use it as I showed above to identify issues with people or groups, BE CAREFUL who sees it! There are easily foreseeable ways to damage trust if somebody finds out they are seen as a "restraining force." By all means use the tool, as you must do something about these issues, but be prudent in discussions of such issues outside the team.

- **Cost/Benefit Analysis**
  Purpose: This tool balances resources required to do something versus the value of that achievement. Resources may include wages or hours of those involved, costs of materials used, any purchases, etc. Value may be measured in sales, costs, efficiency, capability, reduced defect level, etc. In predictive mode, it estimates whether something is worth doing. Used again at the end of an improvement effort, it can be used to validate the actual costs, savings, and total benefit.

How it Works: As I didn't teach project planning under Action Plan, I don't intend to teach accounting here. The purpose, above, pretty much explains the required process. List all the resources you will need to accomplish your goal. List all the benefits that will come from your work. Add measures to them that can be translated into your desired currency (yen, dollars, pounds, etc.) or at least a capability that can be exploited for savings or revenue. In many cases, the benefit—especially if it is now a permanent part of the process—may be annualized. Now subtract the costs from the benefits. If the number is negative, either do something else or find more compelling evidence of value.

Why it Works: Again brutally simple—this can be used both to say what you are going to do and to prove it. It is especially important to get honest data about the financial impact/value of improvement efforts to management, sponsors, executives, etc. This is the data they will rely on to decide how much to support such efforts. That support will greatly affect the speed and/or the direction of the organization's Improvement Engine.

Pitfalls: Don't lie. Don't fudge. Don't spin. If people lose confidence in whether you in particular or the organization in general is capable of deciding whether something is worth doing, they will have little reason to have confidence in much else.

Reflection:

- Reflection here is the same as in the first "What to Do" chapter, with an added caution: human emotions are now involved, and that makes things trickier. You will probably face some internal conflicts in fully adapting these new aspects of the Engine yourself. Be prepared.

- Review this chapter and select a few (2 for the hesitant, 5 for the aggressive) of these points to turn into personal learning assignments. Set a learning plan for yourself, and start applying those techniques. Add more when you are ready.

Chapter 10

Driving the Engine (Leadership)

I have already written two entire chapters on actions to take in order to best manage your Improvement Engine. Leadership, however, deserves its own chapter. In fact, leaders might be a bit overwhelmed at this point by all the things that I have said should be done. *Relax.* There's a lot to do and some perspectives to change, but step back and look at the big picture. Many of the actions I have already recommended are tactical and should thus be executed at lower levels of the organization. This chapter will help leaders focus on the actions/behaviors that will optimize the strategic management of the Engine.

Previously, I have organized my "how to" chapters around specific actions. This chapter will deal instead with areas of emphasis, focusing more on what must be accomplished than the specific methods for doing so. The recommended actions may be a bit less specific, but that is appropriate for a leadership focus; it gives leaders flexibility in deciding how to achieve the desired results. I will explore five basic areas of emphasis:

1) Exemplary Leadership
2) Measurement
3) Meetings

4) Learning
5) The Optimal Bureaucracy

Remember that the Improvement Engine is a management model, not just an improvement model. Leadership and improvement are not just compatible, they are identical. The Engine is more than just an improvement roadmap; it is also a compass.

A note before we begin; some of this chapter repeats points made elsewhere in this book. There are two reasons for this. First, repetition aids learning. Second, I am writing this chapter, to some degree, so that leaders could benefit from reading <u>only</u> this chapter. I surely do not recommend this, as I believe the philosophical foundations of this book set out in the earlier chapters are important to understanding. However, I would like this chapter to have a "stand-alone" feel to it.

- ***Exemplary Leadership***

The point should be obvious; leaders are completely responsible for an organization's culture and its performance. Whatever the organization is or does, it is traceable back to its leaders. The key causal factors here are equally obvious:

1) People imitate leaders, as they are obviously patterns of success in the organization.
2) People assume that leaders' behaviors reflect organizational values.

I have shown that trust is not just part of culture—that it also has a clear impact on performance. No leader would argue that he or she is not responsible for managing performance. Well, then, that means that leaders are responsible for managing the level of trust in an organization as well. Leaders, I tell you this clearly and plainly. First and foremost, the thing which your people must trust is <u>you</u>.

As I said, the point should be obvious. If it is, however, there seem to be a lot of leaders in this world ignoring that point. Most workers—or in the case of governments, citizens—have on many occasions experienced the reverse, primarily in two arenas: intimidation and inconsistency. Far too frequently, leaders use fear to motivate, yet they expect loyalty. They expect mounds of justification for decisions from below, yet they expect their decisions to be obeyed without question. They talk about an organization's values or principles, but then they conspicuously violate them. They tread too close—or even past—the limits of ethical behavior with specious justifications which they would not tolerate from others. They punish failure and non-compliance without regard to purpose or justification. It all comes in several flavors, but those flavors have this in common; too often, leaders do not do what they say.

There are four primary focus areas for trust-building by leaders in order to enable the organization's optimal success:

1) Customers, who must be able to trust that the organization provides product or service according to agreed-upon expectations and at a satisfactory level of cost/value.

2) Employees, who must be able to trust in a consistent pattern of principle and behavior at all levels. They must also trust in leadership's consideration of their well-being. Too often, leadership takes liberties with assumptions about people's capabilities that they would never dream of taking with regard to facilities, equipment, products, etc. The assumption on execution is coached in terms like, "Our people will rise to the challenge". The reality is that they usually just suck it up and trudge on in the face of what seem impossible challenges. In fact, they are often used to cover for the organization's inadequacies.

3) Shareholders, who must be able to trust the organization's responsible management of their investment.

4) Each other. The job of the leadership team is to define purpose, principle, and direction. They cannot do this with any level of consistency if they do not trust one another.

In each of the four remaining focus areas I will discuss, you must consider, in every word and action, the example you set for the organization you lead. Leadership, to be trustworthy, must set and hold itself accountable to principles, and the principles themselves must be trustworthy as well. The past couple of decades have seen a lot of companies devising mission statements and values. Too often, this is an empty exercise that becomes the object of sarcasm and ridicule as the organization comes to understand its hypocrisy. The clear statement of mission and values should not be regarded as a "soft" exercise. Like a national constitution, such articulations of principle should be the guideposts for every member of the organization. Principles define direction when procedure and process are insufficient, as they inevitably will be on occasion. They enable the organization's decision making.

The criteria for selecting—and retaining—leaders should be based at least as much on adherence to principle as it is on performance. Leaders who fail to live up to the standards of such principles should be counseled, marginalized, or, in the final degree, terminated. In particular, there should be no tolerance for those who manage and motivate through fear. If such leaders are getting results, it is a reflection of the capability of the group, not the leader. (If you have problems with that last statement, by the way, return to Chapter 8 and review the impact of fear on the Improvement Engine.)

Finally, beware the exercise of privilege and whim. These are often the foundation for perceived inconsistency in leadership. Be especially careful about that exercise in the context of the organization's systems and procedures. It is somewhat natural and inevitable that people executing those procedures and systems will attach priority to the requests of leaders, and certainly the decisions and directions of leadership often require priority. When leaders demand priority for trivialities, however, the organization's members will—quite correctly— perceive the double standard involved, and they will recognize that the organization's capability is reduced as members must put those trivialities ahead of obviously more important matters. Additionally, if leaders never expose themselves to the natural performance level of the organization's systems, they cannot understand the inefficiencies and obstacles inherent in those systems. A last point about privilege and whim is in the necessity for leaders to explain themselves. The "don't ask questions, just do what I told you" approach to leadership disables learning, crippling the foundation of your Engine.

- ***Measurement***

There are three basic principles involved here:

1) You can't manage what you don't measure (thank you, Dr. Deming). Without measurement, management is arbitrary and more a matter of guesswork than reason.
2) Measurement drives behavior. People will respond to the way they are measured, as they perceive (quite naturally and correctly) doing so as the way to success.
3) Measurement systems are both explicit and implicit. The explicit system is the formal system, defined by procedure and policy. The implicit system is defined by the actual organizational reaction to performance.

First of all, then, you must ensure that you have a measurement system that gives you visibility on your actual success—and what contributes to that success. This means defining measurement systems for both the critical outputs and the critical inputs to your processes. A general guideline here is to pay attention to and prioritize the measurements that predict and/or indicate accomplishment versus activity. This concept was a major part of the turn to quality emphasis in the last part of the 20th century. Previously, organizations tended to focus on the quantity of work done (activity) in order to define productivity. An emphasis on quality gave a more rational balance to measurement, as customer satisfaction (accomplishment) gained more importance and the impact of quality on profitability (a better measure of accomplishment than simple revenue) became better understood. Another key factor to be considered here is the management of how much is measured (always remember that measurement has a cost) and what level of beneficial control is obtained through such measurement. This has much to do with the "optimal bureaucracy," and I will discuss it more fully under that topic.

Secondly, you must give critical and continuing consideration to how measurement will affect behavior. The concept of balancing metrics is crucial here. Too much emphasis on any one metric—even customer satisfaction itself—will inevitably eventually damage an organization's ability to satisfy its customers. Make sure that your organization understands and is correctly motivated by its measurement system. It's OK for those measurements to occasionally change in priority, but the foundation of the measurement system should be relatively stable and well aligned with the values of the company. A key question here, if you want to emphasize the importance of learning in your organization, should be, "Does my measurement system value my intellectual resources?"

Finally, remember that leadership defines the real measurement system by the way it reacts to actual performance. This is the implicit measurement system, and whatever the explicit system may be, it is the implicit system that will drive behavior. Principles, measurement, performance, and behavior are all inextricably intertwined. Leadership reaction to measurement defines whether that mix is synergistic or inconsistent and unproductive.

- **Meetings**

Every meeting is a class in leadership for those involved. There is more cultural learning in meetings than you will ever get from classroom education, as meetings are where leadership is on display. Nowhere is it more important for leaders to recognize their influence as behavioral examples than in meetings.

Make meetings important. Emphasize decision making instead of status reviews; end the "dog and pony show" perception of meetings. Create and hold to agendas. Start meetings on time; treat them as commitments. Ensure that participation by all involved is planned and structured as part of the meeting. Use processes and tools to make decisions. Treat people and ideas with respect. All of these things will contribute not only to better meetings but to corresponding better behavior and performance outside meetings as well. An organization's culture is best reflected in its meetings. Perhaps it is even a result of those meetings. Be relentless in the pursuit of excellent meetings.

- *Learning*

The earliest chapters of this book made it clear that learning is at the foundation of an organization's ability to succeed. Leadership in this arena is crucial, and a focus on the future is necessary to manage learning. Elliott Jacques, a highly controversial figure in management philosophy, describes a concept called "decision horizon" which I think is useful here. Simply stated, decision horizon is the length of time between the present and the time when current decisions will affect the organization's purpose and performance. Supervisors should be making the decisions that affect short-term performance; executives should be making the decisions that affect long-term performance. Thus the lower ranks of management should be most concerned with execution to meet current objectives, while executives should focus more on strategy and the development of capability to meet future needs.

Delegation is a key issue here, and delegation requires trust. If the upper levels of management find themselves continually focusing on execution, that is a key indicator that they have failed to teach their subordinates how to manage. If they cannot trust their subordinates to make the right decision, then they have either failed in managing their subordinates' learning, or they have simply chosen the wrong people. A successful learning strategy should extend the decision horizon of leadership, as they can rely on the organization to accurately assess and respond to current, tactical issues while they focus on the future.

Effective learning does not necessarily correlate with a large training budget. In the final analysis, classroom training is one of the least effective learning methods. It is frequently difficult to actually apply learning to current work in a classroom environment, and without application, training is waste. Leading a learning process is more a matter of emphasizing the need to change behavior and providing opportunity to practice that new behavior than it is a matter of funding. Usually, it is so-called "soft skill" training that suffers here. Technical training is usually recognized as necessary, and the opportunity to apply it is usually immediate. "Soft" skills training, however, often loses its impact simply because there is no real follow-up from management to be sure that those skills get used. The keys here are relatively simple:

1) Define, and continually reexamine, how the organization needs to improve and what learning is necessary, in both technical and cultural terms.
2) Create learning processes outside the classroom (I particularly recommend mentoring) that reinforce new learning.
3) Make the application of new learning a key factor in evaluating performance at all levels.

All leadership needs to be <u>actively</u> involved in this. Relegating all of an organization's learning decisions to a Human Relations or Training department makes the same mistake as relegating the entire responsibility for quality to a Quality department. The names may match, but those departments cannot actually guarantee whether learning is applied or quality is achieved. The real actions that lead to learning or improved quality lie in the hands of those who execute, not in the hands of those who teach or those who inspect, monitor, and report.

Leaders themselves need to be seen as learners—a difficult proposition for those who wish to be seen as infallible. A key component of learning is in understanding where performance needs to be improved. A key cultural factor in doing this successfully is the ability to admit weakness and even failure—and learn from it. Trust plays a major role here, as such admissions are far less likely to come forward in an environment of blame and mistrust.

Learning needs to be everybody's responsibility, and so does teaching. Make clear to every member—from the interview process on—that this is part of your organization's value system. End knowledge hoarding. Recognize and reward the transfer of knowledge. Make this a key aspect of evaluating performance.

- ### *The Optimal Bureaucracy*

The word "bureaucracy" does not have favorable connotations. A certain level of bureaucracy, however, is necessary to successfully manage and execute. The key is to achieve the best balance between creativity and control, which tend rather naturally to bump up against each other. Thinking "outside the box" is, after all, a key component of creativity, while control is a continual effort to clearly define the box. It's a lot like the old example of the weapons manufacturer with one organization working on bullet-proof armor while the other works on armor-piercing projectiles.

Purpose and process share much of the same conflict. Purpose results from creative vision, while process results from the effort to define actions to achieve that vision. Ideally, this should be a symbiotic relationship, as each represents a different side of the Improvement Engine. Principles, purpose, and creativity come from the Invent side of the Engine, but they are pointless without execution, process, and control, which are the products of the Application side.

There is an Old Trainers' Story that beautifully illustrates the process by which many bureaucracies develop. A woman and her husband are working in the kitchen together to prepare dinner. As the husband works on the salad, the wife starts on a family specialty: pot roast.

She begins by taking a large cut of meat and slicing off one end. She then continues with spicing and preparing the roast for the oven. The husband has watched this procedure many times during their married lives, but this time a question strikes him.

"Honey, why do you cut off the end of the roast? I mean, I know we use the tip later for soup, but we could easily eat more roast."

She stops to think a moment, then says, "Well, that's the way my mother taught me, and we've always loved her roast."

He considers this answer a moment, but the question has him going. He asks, "OK, why did your mother cut the end off?"

A little exasperated, she says, "Well, I can't know that, can I? Would you like me to call her and find out?"

Realizing he is pushing his luck, her husband can nonetheless not contain his curiosity. He responds, "Actually, if you don't mind, yes I would."

The wife decides to humor him and calls her mother to ask the purpose of the roast-cutting. Her mother only increases the mystery with her response: "Darling, I really don't have a particular reason. That's the way your grandmother taught me to cook roast."

Now the wife's curiosity is on a par with her husband's. They decide to call her grandmother. She chuckles a bit before answering, "Dear, I only had a little pot to cook it in. Don't tell me you're still doing it that way?"

This story is used to point out our frequent tendency to do things the way we have always done them without seriously questioning the reasons. A participant in a class I was teaching recently (thank you, Sonia Abreu!) made a marvelous point after hearing this story. She pointed out that too often, when a process has problems, we simply create another rule to avoid those problems instead of fixing the underlying causes. We become so used to the process that we come to believe that the process is inherently right, and any poor performance that results must be a failure in execution. In short, we come to believe that our processes are sacred. This is a major error in perception. It is not the process that is sacred, but the <u>purpose</u> of the process, as defined by its customer, and these are entirely different issues.

A final issue about the battle between control and creativity is that rigid control systems can inhibit productive change. If the bureaucracy around justifying and approving changes becomes too burdensome, those with creative ideas will lose trust in the system's ability to value their creative contribution. The amount of justification and approval required becomes emotionally equivalent, in the eyes of those promoting change, to a systematic suspicion of all change on the part of the organization. People just give up; they perceive the effort as not worth the benefit.

Find the balance. Encourage excellence in both creativity and control, and pay particular attention to trust issues where the two conflict. You need two basic structures for this: systems (procedures, measurement, etc., *ala* Baldridge or ISO) and purpose/vision/values. In addition, you need two basic capabilities: execution (especially relative to systems) and leadership (especially relative to purpose, vision and values). Make creativity and control partners in success.

I would like to make a final point about creativity and leadership, and it may seem to conflict with some of what I have said before, but the job of leadership is, at the end of the day, to manage such contradictions. I have stated that learning should extend executive decision horizons. As leaders make decisions that affect more and more distant futures, instinct matters. Yes, I know I have said that decisions should be supported by data, but quite frankly, it is often the "gut instinct" of leaders that finally differentiates where valid choices were made about such distant futures. Vision equates with imagination, and imagination has few statistically meaningful components. Make such decisions carefully, and discuss them at length so that your organization understands the imaginative basis for them.

- **Reflection:**

As with the previous "how to" chapters, reflection is brief. I can put it in one question:

Now that you know the criteria, how do you measure up?

Chapter 11

What I Told You

"Don't let it end like this. Tell them I said something."
Pancho Villa (last words)

I wrote this book because I thought I had come to understand something important. I hope you have discovered something in your reading of it as well. Discovery is the first step in learning, after all, and if there is anything I have tried to communicate in these pages, it is the value of learning. Without learning, there can be no improvement, not in our jobs, not in our government, not in our culture, and not in our lives. Without the promise of learning, hope itself vanishes, and that is not a condition I wish to contemplate or endure.

My primary discovery was a simple model—the Improvement Engine. From that I developed the system of equations I call the Physics of Success. Together, I believe they create a rational model of my own most profound values, and I believe that model fills a gap in the world of thinking around decision making, continuous improvement, and leadership. It seemed to me that improvement and decision making were too often presented as procedural recipes—a list of actions to be copied and repeated. Leadership philosophies seemed to lack procedure altogether, leaving the student of such philosophies with a lot of good ideas but no method to implement them and no model to analyze or predict their effectiveness. This has not always been the fault of the creators. I think especially of Deming and Shewhart's work when I say this. The world of continuous improvement as we understand it today is traceable to the PDCA (Plan, Do, Check, Act) model which they developed somewhere between them. In my opinion, however, too many practitioners have simply "proceduralized" that thinking without integrating the philosophical underpinnings which are, I believe, crucial to the optimal application of those ideas. PDCA, and/or its Six Sigma descendant, DMAIC (Define, Measure, Analyze, Improve, Control), are generally well accepted. Deming's Fourteen Points, however, are less so, yet they are key to the successful implementation of his methods. It is the points, however, not the process, that explain the human element necessary to improvement. These concepts have too often been debated or dismissed as "fuzzy" and "soft" thinking. They are not. They are the throttle on our Improvement Engine, they have profound effects on its performance, and they must be acknowledged and managed. Ultimately, application of the Engine must, in order to be effective, be guided toward doing 2 things:

1) Reducing decision cycle time . . . .
   while

2) Improving decision quality.

The more good decisions you make, and the faster you make them, the more successful you will be.

I have sought, then, to create a simple, graphic model that can be used to understand method as well as motivation. It provides, I believe, a model that elevates continuous improvement method to an integrated model for management itself. The single most significant element of that elevation lies in the inclusion of the words "trust" and "respect" in the model. These are the human factors, and I believe I have demonstrated clear cause and effect cases for paying attention to these as key elements in the pursuit of progress and success.

What, then, have I told you? I think most of it can be wrapped up in the discussion of two words: "learning" and "trust." I will make my points here as succinct as possible.

- ### *Learning*

Learning is a necessary component for improvement. Improvement is necessary to progress. Progress is crucial to long-term success.

Training is not learning. It is only a first step in learning. Application of learning, and the motivation to apply the learning in the first place, are leadership responsibilities which deserve far more attention than they are usually given.

People learn best when they trust the knowledge/information they are given and trust the source/person who delivers it.

Learning is an irrepressible human process. The good news is that a strong and healthy improvement process is at work right now in your organization; and the organization is getting better—but better at what? The Improvement Engine is always running. The secret to success is in making sure that the Engine's direction matches the goals and values of the organization and in ensuring that those goals and values are both motivational and ethically sound in terms of the organization's responsibilities to its customers, its members, and its stakeholders.

- ### *Trust*

Trust and respect go hand in hand, and they relate directly to the speed with which decisions are made in an organization. As such, they are crucial factors in the cycle time of every organizational process.

Fear damages trust. As a motivational technique, it is both short-sighted and distracting, as extended fear suppresses creativity and learning or diverts that creativity and learning to ends that are counter-productive.

Measurement can support trust by providing the data necessary to objective decision making. Because measurement is a motivator, it can also damage trust if it encourages untrustworthy behavior. Remember that the implicit measurement system, as defined by the organization's reaction to measurements, has more effect on behavior than the explicit system defined by policy and procedure. Inconsistencies between the two are breeding grounds for distrust.

You must find the optimal balance of creativity and control, making them—as much as possible—synergistic instead of conflicting. Pay particular attention to the bureaucracy around approving and implementing change. People will cease to trust that the organization values their ideas if the path to change is viewed as a series of bureaucratic obstacles.

Leaders are responsible for managing trust. The better the example they set in this regard, the higher the level of trust in the organization, and thus the higher the level of performance.

• *Summary*

If much of what I have said seems to make plain sense to you, perhaps it is because models are simply a way of representing what we already in some way understand. It is important to find that representation, though—to make it something that can be communicated and discussed. The Improvement Engine makes both of those possible. It is a way to both learn from the past and analyze the probabilities of the future. It integrates the subjective, emotional side of the organization with the objective, rational side.

As a species, we are like super heroes, endowed with powers to literally change the world. Most of us are inspired to use those powers for good. Most of us seek a world of peace and prosperity for all, and hope and trust are the foundation of that vision. We are all customers of each other, as we do, in fact have expectations of each other. This book is my small attempt to contribute to that vision. Thank you for listening.

• *Reflection:*

Enough reflection, I say! Don't just think about it! Do it! Start now.

References and Notes
(in order as they appear in this book)

Clarke, Arthur C. <u>2001: A Space Odyssey</u>. New York: New American Library, 1968.

When I mentioned this book in the foreword, I wasn't really thinking of it as a reference, *exactly. However, it must be said that the book is all about transformational change. Maybe it deserves a look in this context.*

Ouchi, William. <u>Theory Z</u>. White Plains: Addison-Wesley Publishing Co., 1981.

This book was the first "business" book I think I ever read. It was quite popular at the time, and its concepts were well known enough that, in general conversation with business folk, simply saying "Theory Z" was sufficient to communicate a multitude of meanings. It was the first book that I remember to really gain traction in promoting the idea of "listen and lead" vs. "command and control" styles of management.

Senge, Peter. <u>The Fifth Discipline</u>. New York: Currency Doubleday, 1990.

If the only concept discussed in this book were the idea of a "learning organization," it would still be worth reading. It proposes systematic ways of looking at how processes and people interact, and it makes plain the need, especially in the volatile conditions of modern markets, to always *be learning.*

Romig, Dennis. <u>Breakthrough Teamwork</u>. Chicago: Irwin Publishing, 1996.

The best data and conclusions on human performance in organizations.

Romig, Dennis. <u>Side By Side Leadership</u>. Marietta: Bard Press, 2001.

The principles of Breakthrough Teamwork applied to leadership, plus new data and a flexible model for leadership capabilities. Shows that there are many aspects of leadership that are, in fact, very learnable skills with specific actions.

Deming, W. Edwards. <u>Out of the Crisis</u>. Cambridge: Massachusetts Institute of Technology for Advanced Engineering Study, 1982.

It's long and sometimes, frankly, a bit tedious. Read it anyway. Deming had it all right. I hope I have given some new voice to what he meant. This book shows, from the 50-foot to the 50,000-foot level, how leadership and measurement combine to streamline—or barricade—the path to success.

Argyris, Chris. <u>Overcoming Organizational Defenses: Facilitating Organizational Learning</u>. Upper Saddle River: Prentice Hall, 1990.

The only thing I really mentioned about Argyris's work was the Ladder of Inference. The power of that model, however, and even the title of the work in which it was put forward, should tell you that there is much valuable insight in his writings about the behavior of people in groups. Worth a read.

Maslow, Abraham. <u>Motivation and Personality</u>. New York: Harper and Row, 1954.

As with Argyris, I only mentioned one part of Maslow's work, but it is an important one. His "hierarchy of needs" helps in understanding what motivates decisions along Argyris's Ladder of Inference. People will tend in any situation, to put basic physical needs (food, air, sex, etc.) at a high priority. It is not until these needs have been at least minimally met that a person will start thinking about other, higher needs. Maslow proposes four subsequent and basically sequential levels of need: safety is next, followed by love/belonging, esteem, and, at the top of the pyramid, self-actualization (creativity, morality, problem solving, etc.). Ignorance of this concept is a great way to get Engines running amok.

Covey, Stephen M. R. <u>The Speed of Trust</u>. New York: Free Press, 2006

This is a simply marvelous book that explains clearly and obviously why trust and cycle time are joined at the hip, with the added useful point that this also affects costs. Everything in it just makes sense—did to me, anyway.

Liker, Jeffrey. The Toyota Way. New York: McGraw Hill, 2003.

Like Deming's <u>Out of the Crisis</u>, this book shows how a fully integrated management philosophy affects performance. If Deming's concepts were pointed toward listening to data and reducing variation, the basics of what became Six Sigma, then this book, in focusing on eliminating waste and optimizing flow, is pointed toward "Lean" concepts. This is a foundational work in what (I hope) will become the next generation of improvers, working seamlessly between the two major philosophies—and any others that help accomplish the basic goal of designed improvement.

Brassard, Michael. <u>The Memory Jogger: A Pocket Guide of Tools for Continuous Improvement</u>. Salem: Goal/QPC, 1985.

This was the first in what turned out to be a long series of <u>Memory Jogger</u> titles; there are <u>Memory Joggers</u> for Six Sigma, for Lean, for Teams . . . the list is quite extensive. They are consummately handy things, designed to fit in a shirt pocket. Each usually contains brief, clear explanations, with examples, of how to use tools for all phases of decision making. Additionally, there is usually a matrix in the front to help one decide what tool to use in a given situation. No serious improver should be without at least one.

The Improvement Engine Workbook

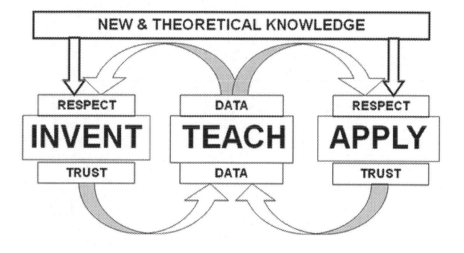

As You Get Started...

This workbook has been designed to enhance your study of Matt Rollins' life work. His major professional legacy comes to you in the form of 3 key components:

- The Improvement Engine
- The Physics of Success
- Using both in Workbook form to create "mini Matt's"—improvement and trust engineers

With Matt's message being delivered in an intense, scientific manner, I ask that you treat it as the simple core content that Matt Rollins was so famous for. Because it is in the understanding and friction of complexity versus simplification that the answer to success is sparked!

This workbook is intended to help you "learn" about your current organization and to help you use the knowledge of an executive leadership or other organizational team to propel your organization to mind-blowing success! Although there may be benefit in going through this Workbook alone, it is designed to go through as a team over a series of weeks (perhaps one chapter and workbook section per week – approximately 1 to 2 hours each week).

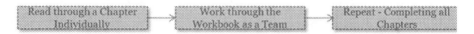

Executive leadership teams going through this process allowing for discussions and consensus decision making can expect to:

- Justify, for yourself and others, an increasingly passionate fixation on learning as the foundation of sustainable success.

- Acknowledge and plan for the fact that few – if any – changes of a meaningful nature are accomplished without some change of human behavior. In order to accomplish improvement, project and process improvement leaders must change people as well as products, processes, and services.
- Take specific, justifiable actions (several will be suggested) to increase the pace and quality of learning and improvement.
- Use the Engine as an analytical tool to discover what systemic factors are supporting or hindering your efforts to improve.
- Adjust – or build from scratch if necessary – a leadership philosophy, with corresponding actions, which comprehends the above and maximizes the results achieved thereby.

Now, let's begin the process of demystifying *The Improvement Engine* and The Physics of Success...

Chapter 1
What I'm Going to Tell You

What does continuous improvement mean to this organization? Be sure to include both the positives and negatives about how continuous improvement is perceived.

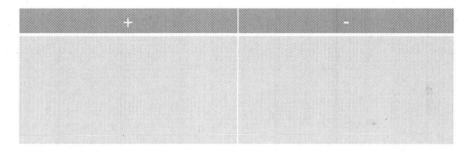

+	-

How would you like the organization to perceive continuous improvement?

What are the 3 best and worst things your own department/organization has done in trying to make a change, complete a project, etc. – an activity that involved (perhaps depended upon) the input/work of others. Write these experiences down. Be prepared to share 1 of each with the group.

Best Personally	Worst Personally
1.	1.
2.	2.
3.	3.

Brainstorm the 3 best and 3 worst examples your entire company/ organization/division/ location has of successful and failed opportunities/ projects/efforts? Note, these do not have to be from the previous items (those were from departments – although some may be repeated).

Best Personally	Worst Personally
1.	1.
2.	2.
3.	3.

Come to a consensus on which 1 of the BEST and 1 of the WORST can be utilized as you go through The Improvement Engine Workbook.

• BEST:

• WORST:

Determine what you want to be able to do better, as a team, as a result of reading this book.

•
•
•
•
•

Chapter 2
Change, Learning, and Improvement

Is the following true?

Improvement = Change

Yes/No? Provide company/organization examples to support your position.

What must be added?

Improvement = Change + _____

Discuss the possible four scenarios, of this suggested equation, and provide examples for each:

- An unfavorable change occurs, and nobody learns how or why (change and learning are both negative). Obviously there is no improvement here.
  Example:

- A favorable change occurs, but nobody learns how or why (change positive, learning negative). This is a happy accident, but without learning, it is likely to be erased since nobody understands how to sustain the change. This can be called improvement only so far as the favorability of the change outweighs and/or outlasts the failure to learn from it.
  Example:

- An unfavorable change occurs, but the root cause is discovered (change negative, learning positive). Since the root cause is discovered, the unfavorable change may be reversed. Also, understanding of the root cause can lead to predictive planning, so that such unfavorable changes may be better anticipated and prevented in the future. In most cases, this is more productive and sustainable than the kind of possible improvement under scenario 2.
  Example:

- A favorable change occurs, and there is substantial knowledge about how and why (change and learning are both positive -- this would especially apply in the case of successful, planned changes). When positive change is accompanied by learning, there can be no doubt that improvement has been achieved.
  Example:

Improvement requires change combined with learning.

Improvement = Change + Learning

Learning is the more overlooked and possibly the more important of these two elements.

What are the learning systems in your organization?

Do you rely primarily on classroom training? Why or why not?

Are there opportunities to improve the quality of learning simply by using alternative methods such as coaching or mentoring?

Are supervisors, managers, and executives measured on their ability to develop the capabilities of their staff?

Are they expected to <u>rigorously</u> ensure that new learning has a chance to be immediately practiced?

Do their immediate superiors highlight occasions when new learning by their staff will require change of behavior (e.g., modeling the behavior or leading execution of new techniques) by that staff's supervision?

Is learning carefully considered and designed as a part of each project?

Is the same rigor applied to that planning as to the listing and scheduling of required activities?

Change is a powerful, chaotic force just as likely to destroy as to build. It is natural to fear and/or resist change to some degree. Answer the following questions about you personally, and then about the organization/company as a whole. Be prepared to discuss openly and honestly.

What is your own attitude toward change?

- Personally
- Organizationally

Recognizing that improvement absolutely requires change, do you comfortably accept that change will never end if you seek a state or outcome better than today's?

- Personally
- Organizationally

It is often easy to recognize when change would benefit systems, products, and other people's performance or attitudes.

- Personally
- Organizationally

How good are you at recognizing – and accepting and pursuing – change that is required of you in beliefs, habits, and actions?

- Personally
- Organizationally

Learning is the assimilation of knowledge to support change in behavior.

Learning = Communication + Application

Communication must be measured by its result, not its intent. Learning, as it has communication as one of its components, must also be measured by its result, not its intent.

Does "Learning = Communication + Application" match your experience? Provide examples.

Should learning and change be the components of improvement?

Complete the following SWOT (Strengths, Weaknesses, Opportunities, and Threats) Analysis in order to identify change opportunities in your organization.

SWOT Analysis	
Strengths • • •	**Weaknesses** • • •
Opportunities • • •	**Threats** • • •

Circle the two items that need the most immediate attention. What are the actions that could be put in place immediately to begin to make progress on these items?

#	Action	Owner	Estimated Completion Date
1			
2			
3			

What changes (if any) should be put in place to create a better "learning" environment?

-
-
-
-

As a result of The Improvement Engine discussions so far, what, if anything, should you start or stop doing inside of the organization? When should this happen? Who will do it?

-

-

Chapter 3
The Physics of Success

In the pursuit of success, it is tempting to focus on that which is most easily understandable (e.g., controlling costs, building revenue, executing activities according to a timeline, etc.). The equations of the Physics of Success make plain, however, that none of these things actually happen without a foundation of learning, change, and improvement.

Are your organization's energies properly focused, in light of this conclusion? Why or why not?

How well can your organization adapt to the fact that some of its most important energies must be expended on that which is difficult or impossible to measure?

Think of a major project in your organization that succeeded. How do you see these equations played out in the way the project was initiated, managed, executed, and finalized?

Improvement = Change + Learning
Learning = Communication + Application

Repeat the last question for a project that failed.

Vision is the harness that directs improvement into the path of progress.

Does your organization have a clearly articulated vision? Does that vision include mission and values? (If yes, take out your vision, mission, and values and review.)

If there is a vision, is it really, honestly inspiring?

Have you ever actually referred to it to make a decision about how or whether to do something?

Beyond the hype, "continuous improvement" and "learning organization" are still important terms representing vital components of sustainable success. Define both terms, as you would like them to be perceived, for your organization:

- Continuous improvement
- Learning organization

Discuss the following as a formula to be added to the Physics of Success. Can you have progress without improvement?

Is improvement all you need for progress?

Progress = Improvement

So what must be added to improvement to turn it into progress?

The answer, as implied above, has something to do with direction, does it not?

Progress = Improvement + Vision

Vision is the imagined state of the organization at some future point: its size, its wealth, its influence, the nature and needs of its customers, etc. Mission is the activity on which the organization will focus in order to achieve that vision. Values are the guidelines and boundaries that the organization places on behavior that will be considered acceptable and/or laudable in pursuit of the mission and the vision. In the above equation, please include mission and values as parts of vision. Also, assume that vision implies shared vision.

Are your vision, mission, values and improvements aligned?

Why or why not?

What, if anything, needs to be done to establish alignment?

Next, consider the difference in Vision and Shared Vision. Which do you have?

Why is it essential for the Vision to be "shared", and by whom?

What actions if any should take place to ensure your vision is a shared vision?

#	Action	Owner	Estimated Completion Date
1			
2			
3			

So now these three equations tell us that in order to achieve progress, we must focus on rigorously planned learning, couple that with change activities to achieve improvement, and direct that improvement toward an ideal state within behavioral boundaries defined by law, ethics, and our own conscience.

Progress = Improvement + Vision
Improvement = Change + Learning
Learning = Communication + Application

But progress, like improvement, is not an adequate final goal. The history of failed organizations is filled with stories of progress which, through misfortune or mismanagement, proved insufficient to keep the organization alive. The end goal of all this must be what we call "success."

Define success for your organization.

Success = _____

In the Physics of Success, success is defined as follows:

Success = Progress + Profit + Productivity

Does this last formula work for your organization? Why or why not?

Let us look at the entire set of equations, or the Physics of Success:

- **Success = Progress + Profit + Productivity**
- **Progress = Improvement + Vision**
- **Improvement = Change + Learning**
- **Learning = Communication + Application**

Another look at this may be had by adding all the minor components together to achieve the end result:

Success = Communication + Application + Change + Vision + Profit + Productivity

As in the disciplines of physics, a very complex concept, success, is defined by a host of smaller components. Also, as in physics, you must achieve understanding of the lesser components before you can get to the greater. Thus not only the list, but also the order of the above components is important. <u>There is a mathematical relation between success and improvement, and this relationship demands learning as one of its most critical components.</u>

Complete the following template to define success for your organization. Take time to come to a consensus.

Putting the Physics of Success to Work for Your Company/Organization	
Success = Progress + Profit + Productivity	
Define Successful Progress	
Define Successful Profit	
Define Successful Productivity	
Progress = Improvement + Vision	
Define Improvement Needs	
Define a "shared" vision, mission, values and goals that support the above definition of success.	
Agree on roles, responsibilities and linkages that must exist for success.	
Improvement = Change + Learning	
Define Changes Needed	
Define Learning Requirements	
Learning = Communication + Application	
Define Communication Strategy (Teaching)	
Define Application Strategy	

Chapter 4
Building the Improvement Engine

This book only provides you with an Engine and a chassis; you are responsible for the rest of your organizational vehicle.

Finish the vehicle design – at least in your mind. Picture your organization, with its unique values, mission, and resources, running with this Engine under the hood.

What are the attributes or characteristics of your vehicle?

-
-
-
-

If someone from the outside was to describe your organization, how might they describe it?

-
-
-

Let's perform a quick competitive analysis to determine how your customers view your organization. Fill in this template comparing your customers' needs and how you stack up against your competition.

Performance Indicator Compared to the Customer Need		1– Low	2	3	4	5 – High
Customer Need #1	You		X			
	Competitor A			X		
	Competitor B	X				
Customer Need #2	You				X	
	Competitor A			X		
	Competitor B					X
Customer Need #3	You					X
	Competitor A				X	
	Competitor B				X	

Example Competitive Analysis

Performance Indicator Compared to the Customer Need		1 – Low	2	3	4	5 – High
	You					
	You					
	You					

Are there opportunities for improvement?

-
-
-

Learning is an interaction between innovation and implementation.

Who are the innovators in your organization?

-
-
-

Who are the implementers?

-
-
-

Think about them in the context of this model; any insights?

-
-
-

What is the quality of interaction between your innovators and implementers?

Do you see "over the wall syndrome" there?

How well is the process for delivering deployment data defined? What does this mean for your organization?

How well is the process for delivering application data <u>as a learning tool</u> defined? What does this mean for your organization?

Improvement benefits from a "safe" place, supported by data, where innovators and implementers can learn together.

Does your organization have such a place (i.e., do you have trustworthy, objective processes for looking at what's new and what you have done and learning from both)?

Is mutual respect expected, modeled, and reinforced in your organization?

Application data benefits from analysis; deployment data is subject to judgment. How comfortable are you with the subjective nature of "best" choices about innovation?

Would you overturn a deployment choice if you found that a seemingly less logical choice would be better supported – and therefore probably more successfully implemented – by those involved in the process?

Does your organization use reliable, statistical methods for defining data collection plans and analyzing the resulting data?

There is a tremendous amount to be learned from failure.

Does your own experience validate this? What are some failures (or at least some things you could have done better) in your life from which you have gained significant wisdom?

How good are you at identifying and confronting your own weaknesses and/or failures?

What level of "messenger shooting" does your organization experience?

What is the impact on learning, as this book uses that term?

Does your organization have a systematic process for examining itself for weaknesses and failures and learning from them without blame?

How does your organization currently handle lessons learned?

How are lessons learned incorporated into the planning process of the next project?

The first attempt at the Improvement Engine diagram reflected Innovation, Design and Deployment Data and the subsequent activities of Implementation, Experience, and Application Data.

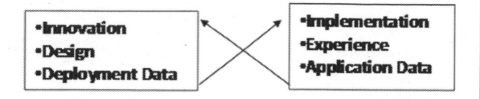

Who performs these tasks in your organization?

What works well and not so well in this part of your organization? Why?

Discuss the handoffs between these organizations.

What could be done better?

One of the next diagrams is what was first called the "learning model."

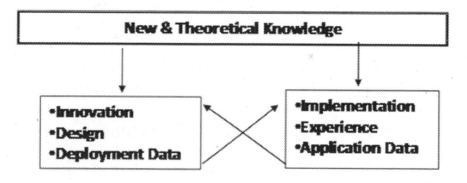

Do you see the cultural change in the light of the Physics of Success?

Can you point to it in the hierarchy of equations?

- **Success = Progress + Profit + Productivity**
- **Progress = Improvement + Vision**
- **Improvement = Change + Learning**

• **Learning = Communication + Application**

The next iteration of the Improvement Engine Model took on this new form:

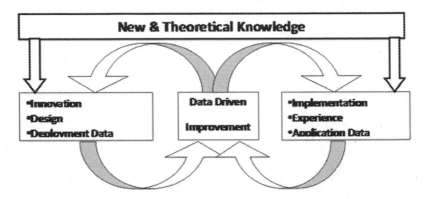

What happens in the center box of the Improvement Engine?

First of all, remember that this Engine is <u>always</u> running. The Engine is running in your organization right now, and your organization is learning new things every second. If that sounds good, wait for the *caveat*: they may not be learning what you would hope. Everyone is learning about each other: whom to talk to, whom to listen to, whom to imitate. Some may even be learning how to build a business just like this, but a bit better... One of an organization's greatest challenges – recognized by the current popularity of the term "alignment" in reference to an organization's goals and actions -- is to maximize the learning of its member that is relevant to the organization's values, vision, mission, and goals.

What is relevant learning in your organization?

- •
- •
- •

What types of data does each of the sides produce?

Is this data treated the same by management? Why or why not?

What data is currently generated that is the most effective in helping you to run your business?

What data is currently being generated that adds little or no value? Should you stop the process of generating this data? Why or why not?

Take a moment to really think how pervasive the effect of these two different environments is.

Chapter 5
What to Do – Part 1

Review the key points of Chapter 5 and choose 1 or 2 for you to focus on personally.

- Take an aggressive stance toward change.
- Change your perspective about what you think of as "communication" – it may be unidentified learning.
- Become an expert at identifying your own and your organization's soft spots.
- Understand learning – in the broad definition of this model – as a critical factor in the cycle time of improvement. Adjust your expectations accordingly.
- Don't use a "course catalog" approach to training. Design appropriate learning strategies for each specific need.
- Keep a critical eye on the flow of new and theoretical knowledge.
- Ensure appropriate preparation for training and follow-up after training.
- Examine processes, projects, and strategies for information hand-offs – identify them as separate learning actions, and use this model to plan them.
- Conduct "pre-learning" exercises before major projects.
- Learn how to state a proper learning objective. Review project plans for required behavior change. Define them as learning objectives, and design appropriate learning for each such change. Focus at least as much on decision making as activity; correct execution depends first on correct decisions.
- Develop structured processes to learn from experience – especially bad experience.
- Examine relationships with suppliers and customers – and even across groups within your own organization – for possible learning opportunities – especially free ones!

Which points will you focus on?

-
-
-
-

What will you do to make progress on these points? Pick a partner and share your strategy for success. Be sure to state what you will do and by when.

- What:
  When:
- What:
  When:

As a team, determine 2 that should be focused on as an entire organization.

-
-

What are short term actions that can be put in place in the next week to make progress? Be sure to list who, what and when of these actions.

#	Action	Owner	Estimated Completion Date
1			
2			
3			
4			
5			
6			

What are long term actions that must be put in place within the next 6 months or longer?

#	Action	Owner	Estimated Completion Date
1			
2			
3			
4			
5			
6			

Chapter 6
Finishing the Improvement Engine

As you continue to look at the Improvement Engine, the processes and people on the left hand side of the diagram will be referred to as Invention and Inventors. The right hand side of the diagram will be referred to as Application and Appliers.

The main point of this whole chapter has been to introduce trust and respect as gating factors to each element of the Improvement Engine – and to thus explain the "human" rationale of continuous improvement.

What is the state of trust and respect in your organization?

If you were to look for specific evidence of each, what would you find, good and bad?

	Good	Bad
Trust		
Respect		

Are employees/members reasonably "safe" in taking independent action as long as such action is clearly in support of the vision/mission and in accordance with values?

How do structures and systems within your organization support or disable trust and respect? (Consider especially systems for evaluating human performance and approving expenditures.)

How do groups within your organization interact?

Are there groups with a known history of mutual suspicion? Why?

How do executives encourage/discourage these suspicions?

How does the executive team interact?

Are they visibly in support of each other, or are they visibly in competition with each other?

What structures and systems within your organization support or disable trust and respect at the executive level?

The simplest way for people to learn to trust each other is to see each other make commitments to do things in support of the other and then to see those commitments kept. – In other words, to see that they can rely on others to do what they say they will do.

What can be done in your organization to create simple, visible ways for individuals and groups to make and keep commitments with each other, starting small and getting progressively bigger?

- Small Ways
  -
  -
- Large Ways
  -
  -

How well does your basic organizational culture value making and keeping commitments?

Start with the concept of "on time." Do meetings start on time?

Are appointments consistently kept?

Are assignments routinely completed on schedule?

Behaviors in each of these areas can send signals that reflect the organizations commitment to commitment itself.

Use the Improvement Engine diagram as a visual prompt to trace reasons for failure and success.

Make a list of three major initiatives that have gone well (if you didn't already do this at the start of the book).

-
-
-

Then, make a list of three major initiatives that have not been successful.

-
-
-

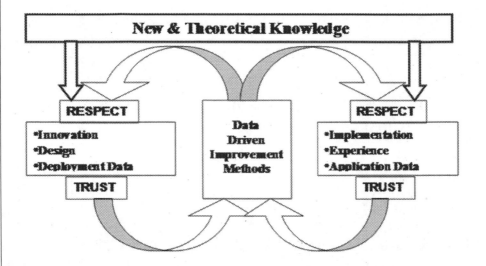

Discuss each of the 3 successful projects/efforts and each of the 3 unsuccessful projects independently. Determine where in the model the success or failure could be attributed.

Here are some questions to consider in this exercise. When you originally experienced these events:

- What information (or misinformation) prompted Inventors to take action? Where did it come from?
- What made the Inventors trust/respect the source (or not)?
- Was the plan/design developed in communication with the Appliers?
- What level of faith did the Inventors have in the ability of the Appliers to understand and execute?
- In meetings among themselves, did Appliers praise or belittle the efforts of the Inventors? To what degree and to what effect? Ask the same questions with regard to Inventors.
- How forthcoming were the Appliers in providing information about their performance, especially the sub-optimal kind?
- Did Appliers do a good job of highlighting the best areas for Inventors to work on for improvement?

- Were Application data subjected to rigorous, objective analysis to produce conclusions that all parties could support (consensus)?
- How much attention did Inventors pay to Applier feedback? How did future plans/designs/actions of the Inventors reflect that?
- What level of respect was evident between leaders of Inventing and Applying organizations?
- How did trust and respect, both of information and those providing it, affect the speed, quality or volume of execution, learning, and improvement?

What is the next most pressing project in your business/organization?

Look at, or consider, the current plan of action for that venture/project. Are there places where trust and respect issues might put the plan at risk?

How can trust be built in advance to reduce risk?

Next, have each organization or role represented answer these questions and post them visibly for everyone to see. Review the posted items 1-by-1 as an entire group. Remember to keep each other's self-esteem intact!

- What characteristics must exist for you to trust a person, data, decision, or process?
- What characteristics must exist for you to respect a person, data, decision, or process?
- What existing organizational data do you trust and why?
- How do you personally like to be approached when it comes to change?

- Which other organization/function in the company is it most critical for your organization to trust and respect?
- What is the one thing you could do differently to increase that trust and respect?
- What is the one thing you would like that other organization to do differently to increase trust and respect?

Note: It is critical to discuss these items honestly. Don't hesitate to pull in facilitation support.

There was one final modification to the improvement engine: the center box has been renamed "Teach".

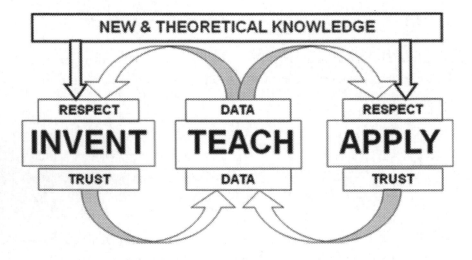

Notice that data is the filter coming into and leading out of the "Teach" box. What implications does this have on an organization?

Where is good data currently lacking from your company's processes?

-
-
-

Where is your company's best data?

-
-
-

Failure's root cause is often found at the interfaces rather than in the 3 primary boxes themselves. Trust, like quality, cannot be an event or a program; it must be institutional, an enduring system of relationships.

Key question: If you are looking to get truly exceptional performance from your Improvement Engine, what should you do?

Chapter 7
Data, Comparison, and Validation

Which continuous improvement model(s) are you currently using?

- Six Sigma
  - DMAIC
  - DMADV
- Lean
- Lean / Six Sigma Combination
- Work Outs
- Plan, Do, Check, Act
- _____
- _____

Trust and respect are enablers of improvement. Therefore, the Improvement Engine can be an overlay, or perhaps even an umbrella, for all of the major continuous improvement methodologies.

How does the Improvement Engine fit with your continuous improvement approach?

What are areas of conflict between the two (if any)?

Should you incorporate the Improvement Engine into your existing approach? If yes, how?

Does the Improvement Engine match with what you believe about behavior, principles, and models that are effective in improving organizational performance?

If not, are the differences trivial or significant?

Are they visible in unique features, or do you feel they represent a real credibility issue for the Engine?

If the Engine does match with your experience and intuition, what new questions can you ask with an understanding of the Engine in hand?

Think of the various groups that make up your organization. What is the role of each in establishing trust in the process and/or trust in results?

Let's examine each of these points.

Thorough
Transparent
Traceable

Thorough – You did all you need to.
Transparent – I know what you did and how.
Traceable – I see why.

Determine processes inside your organization that lack in one or more of the areas Thorough, Transparent, and Traceable.

-
-
-

Determine processes that excel in being Thorough, Transparent, and Traceable.

-
-
-

Are there any organizational needs regarding being Thorough, Transparent, and Traceable? If so, capture needed action items.

#	Action	Owner	Estimated Completion Date
1			
2			
3			
4			
5			
6			

Let's look at several specific points of data from Dr. Romig's <u>Breakthrough Teamwork.</u>

- Employees involved in setting their own work goals achieve better performance.
- Participation increases likelihood of individual action.
- Participation in decisions about performance improved productivity and reduced costs.

- Involvement in planning work changes reduced resistance to changes and increased productivity.
- Teams that develop many creative alternatives make more effective decisions.
- Structured brainstorming methods result in as much as a 100% improvement over unstructured methods.
- Teams using a facilitator to guide brainstorming generated almost 45% more unique ideas than teams not using a facilitator.
- Procedures and structure (in meetings) help groups perform better.
- Groups that use a structured problem-solving process produce more effective solutions.
- Structured group processes improve decision making.
- Structured groups achieve 60% implementation of decisions versus 40% for unstructured groups.
- For a team not trained in a structured decision-making process, 20% of their team's time is spent on disorganized activity for each decision.
- When structured, participative decision-making was used versus direction from a subject matter expert, the cycle time of deciding and implementing ("accomplishment" cycle time) was reduced by 50%.

As a group discuss each of the points. Do you agree/disagree?

Which (if any) should your organization incorporate and/or enhance?

What actions, if any, should be put in place?

#	Action	Owner	Estimated Completion Date
1			
2			

Chapter 8
The Eighth Point

Does your organization use intimidation as a management tool/tactic in the workplace?

Do you?

In your organization, does power make it impossible to object to bad behavior? Explain.

What are the long-term consequences of using fear to motivate short-term accomplishments?

Are there times when using fear as a motivator is okay? Explain.

The use of fear and intimidation, especially as management or "leadership" tools, has the following drawbacks:

- Fear misdirects learning and improvement, thus diverting the Engine's energy to unproductive pursuits.
- As a motivator, fear is more volatile, less predictable, and therefore riskier than kindness or, at least, emotional objectivity.
- "Leadership" by fear is simply less effective and therefore less successful in most circumstances, especially in the long run.
- Using fear to drive people's behavior is based on an inferior moral principle – and people know it.

Do you agree/disagree with these conclusions? Why?

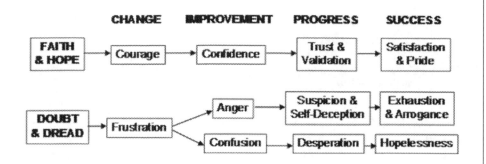

In groups of 3, discuss what happens at each step of the sequence or process. Then, determine examples of each of the 3 paths up the equations that form the Physics of Success. Use these questions to help get you started.

- When we approach **change** with courage what happens? What do we see/witness/hear?
- When we pursue **improvement** with confidence what happens?
- When we validate, it allows us to attach trust to our **progress**. What is the impact?
- When we achieve **success** how do we view the victory (or alleged victory)?
- What is one real world example of this happening in your organization?
- When we approach **change** with frustration what happens? What do we see/witness/hear?
- When we pursue **improvement** with anger what happens?
- When we view **progress** with suspicion and self-deception what happens? What is the impact?
- When we achieve (alleged) **success** in a state of exhaustion and arrogance, how do we view the victory?
- What is one real world example of this happening in your organization?
- When we pursue **improvement** with confusion what happens?
- When we view **progress** with desperation what happens? What is the impact?

- When we achieve (alleged) **success** in a state of hopelessness, how do we view the victory?
- What is one real world example of this happening in your organization?

In your own words, what does the Improvement Engine tell us about the impact of fear?

Do you take longer to act when you fear the consequences? Why or why not?

Ask yourself – very honestly – the following: If people fear the people to whom they give information, what is the likely effect?

The effects of fear, then, as observed through the lens of the Physics of Success, are to:

- heighten the likelihood of wrong choices,
- shorten the organizational horizon, and
- reduce productivity – or at least divert productivity toward unaligned objectives.

The Engine pointed out these further effects:

- Decrease in levels of trust
- Lengthening of cycle times for decision making and, therefore, improvement
- Interference with aligned learning

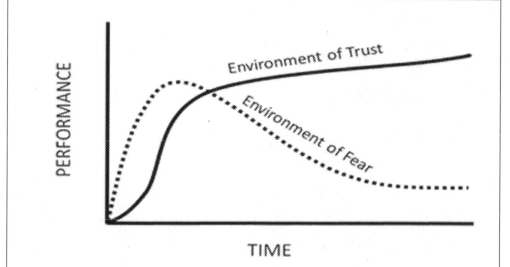

Chapter 9
Metrics and Motives –
Measurements Drive Behavior

What measures/standards (both conscious and subconscious) do you apply to your department?

-
-
-

What measures/standards (both conscious and subconscious) do you apply to other departments within your company/organization?

-
-
-

Are they appropriate and pertinent? Why or why not?

How do you react to what you measure?

Is that reaction consistent with your stated measurement system?

Are there differences between your explicit and implicit measurement systems?

What is meant by explicit and implicit?

What behavior do you expect as a result of what you measure and how you react?

Does your measurement system – including the performance review process – give people a clear picture of their individual performance as well as the group's?

How does your measurement system impact trust between parties involved in events and processes around you?

Brainstorm the measurements that you have in your organization.

-
-
-
-
-
-
-
-
-

Are all of these still needed?

Are there any that could be eliminated?

Are there conflicting measurement systems within the company – especially between organizations/departments and/or individuals?

How is trust impacted when measurement systems conflict?

Key points regarding measurement systems:

- We all have a complex measurement system working within us.
- Our measurements and standards – and those of others – drive our behavior.
- When systems differ or conflict, lack of trust is likely to ensue.
- As organizations, our choices of what to measure and our reactions to those measures should be a matter of the most intense consideration, for they are probably the most influential decisions in defining motivation, culture, and performance.

Take ample time to review your reports, performance expectations, and measures to make sure you as leaders aren't creating distrust in your organization.

Chapter 10
What to Do – Part 2

Using the primary actions recommended in Chapter 5, assess which of these actions will:

- Affect trust?
- Be affected by trust?

Primary Action	Affects Trust	Affected by Trust
Take an aggressive stance toward change.		
Change your perspective about what you think of as "communication" – it may be unidentified learning.		
Become an expert at identifying your own and your organization's soft spots.		
Understand learning – in the broad definition of this model – as a critical factor in the cycle time of improvement. Adjust your expectations accordingly.		
Don't use a "course catalog" approach to training. Design appropriate learning strategies for each specific need.		
Keep a critical eye on the flow of new and theoretical knowledge.		
Ensure appropriate preparation for training and follow-up after training.		
Examine processes, projects, and strategies for information hand-offs – identify them as separate learning actions, and use this model to plan them.		
Conduct "pre-learning" exercises before major projects.		
Learn how to state a proper learning objective. Review project plans for required behavior changes. Define them as learning objectives, and design appropriate learning for each such change. Focus at least as much on decision making as activity; correct execution depends first on correct decisions.		
Develop structured processes to learn from experience – especially bad experience		
Examine relationships with suppliers and customers – and even across groups within your own organization – for possible learning opportunities – especially free ones!		

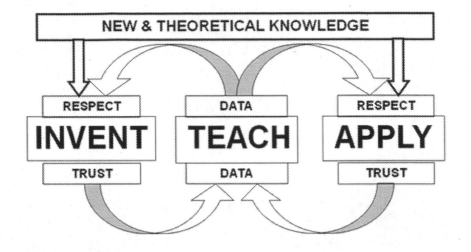

All right, what did you find?

How does an organization's ability to learn – and therefore to develop, and therefore to improve – react to issues of trust?

Can you think of incidents where lack of trust affected your own ability to learn?

Can you think of incidents where lack of trust affected your organization's ability to learn?

-
-
-

Can you also recall incidents where sound relationships and organizational principles contributed to your own, or your organizations, learning?

-
-
-

The people most trusted meet one common description: they do what they say they will do.

There are some specific actions you can take to build trust:

- Assure and emphasize successful completion of early milestones. As people see others meeting commitments, they will not only gain trust in those individuals, they will be motivated to return the favor.
- Establish a few important ground rules for respectful, trustworthy behavior in your organization, and treat them as something close to sacred. (Be careful not to go overboard here. Too many rules will invariably lead to trivialization. Try to make it a list of six or less.)
  - ○
  - ○
  - ○
  - ○
  - ○
  - ○

Examine your meeting culture. What happens in your meetings?

Meetings mirror the values of the organizational cultures. What would a new person see in your meeting mirror in terms of:

- Behaviors
- Meeting commitments
- Interaction
- Expectation for results/accomplishments
- Personal attacks
- Accountability
- Data
- Decision making
- Trust
- Respect

Complete a quick tool review. Divide into pairs. Split the tools up within the groups. Each group should complete the work for their assigned tools. Be prepared to briefly discuss or summarize with the entire group.

Tool	Draw what it looks like	When to use?	Benefits?
Brainstorming			
Voting			
Problem Solving			
SIPOC			
Process Maps or Flow Charts			
Trust Touch			
Summary Statistics and Charts			
Cause & Effect Diagram			
Decision Criteria Matrix			
Action Plan			
Force Field Analysis			
Cost Benefit Analysis			

Chapter 11
Driving the Engine - Leadership

Now that you know the criteria for the Improvement Engine, how do you and your organization measure up? Take ample time to discuss.

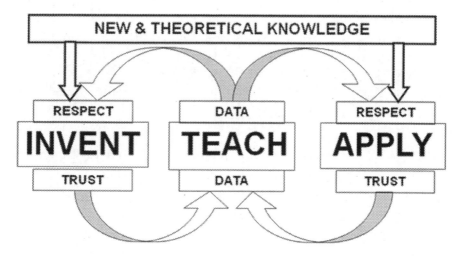

Explore each of the five basic areas of emphasis:

- Exemplary Leadership
  - Whatever the organization is or does, it is traceable back to its leaders. What implications does this have on your organization if any?
  - People imitate leaders, as they are obviously patterns of success in the organization.
    - List good behaviors being imitated.
    - List behaviors being imitated that could use a course correction.
    - What behaviors of today will have to change in order for your organization to adapt to the ever changing global and competitive environment you face?

- People assume that leaders' behaviors reflect organizational values.

  - List leader behaviors in alignment with values.
  - List leader behaviors that should be altered/stopped.

- The thing which your people must trust most is **<u>YOU.</u>**

  - Have you and the other leaders of your organization increased or decreased trust over the last 1-3 years? Discuss examples.

    -
    -
    -

  - What things do your employees need/want to trust you on?

    -
    -
    -

  - What things require you to trust your employees?

    -
    -

  - What is the 1 thing that you could do over the next 6 months to dramatically increase trust in the overall organization?

  - What action items that should be documented regarding trust?

#	Action	Owner	Estimated Completion Date
1			
2			
3			
4			
5			
6			

- Can your customers trust your product or service? Why or why not?

  - What is the one thing you can do to increase customer trust?

- Can your suppliers/business partners trust you? Why or why not?

  - What is the one thing you can do to increase supplier/business partner trust?

- Can your shareholders trust you? Why or why not?

  - What is the one thing you can do to increase shareholder trust?

- Do you as a leadership team, trust one another? Why or why not?

  - What is the one thing that can be done to increase leadership team trust?

- Are there additional action items you need to capture as a Leadership Team?

#	Action	Owner	Estimated Completion Date
1			
2			
3			
4			
5			
6			

- Measurement
  - There are three basic principles involved here:
    - You can't manage what you don't measure.
      - What are the 3 primary measures of your organization's success?
        - ○
        - ○
        - ○
      - How does your customer know if you are successful? Is this reflected in the measurements above?
    - Measurement drives behavior.
      - What good behavior is being driven by your measures?
      - What negative behavior is being driven by your measures?
      - Should you make any adjustments?
    - Measurement systems are both explicit and implicit. (This topic was discussed in a previous chapter.) Add any additional comments or learnings.
  - Leadership defines the real measurement system by the way it reacts to actual performance. Discuss one of your last program or project reviews. What did your behavior relay to the organization?

- Meetings
  - Every meeting is a class in leadership for those involved. Dissect previous all-hands, design/program or project reviews for what is being taught in your meetings.
- Learning
  - How do you reward/recognize the transfer of knowledge? Is this approach working? Why or why not?
  - Do you have pockets of knowledge that would be lost if key talent were no longer in their current roles? What are you doing to minimize this risk?
- The Optimal Bureaucracy
  - A certain level of bureaucracy is necessary to successfully manage and execute.
  - Too much bureaucracy can diminish creative ideas and trust.
  - Articulate the optimal level of bureaucracy you as a leadership team agree on.

Chapter 12
What I Told You

In order to be effective, the Engine must be guided toward doing 2 things:

- Reduce decision cycle time.
  - How can/should you use the Engine to reduce decision cycle time? Allow discussion time and consensus building within the Executive Leadership Team.
- Improve decision quality.
  - How can/should you use the Engine to improve decision quality? Allow time for discussion, and consensus within the Executive Leadership Team.

This workbook on the Improvement Engine and the Physics of Success has been created as a foundation for discussion. The model elevates continuous improvement to an integrated model for leadership itself. The single most significant elements lie in the inclusion of two words: "learning" and "trust". The more times you refer to the Engine, the more and richer your learning. Don't stop with this discussion. Capture your next steps. Recommend you place the next page with The Improvement Engine and The Physics of Success in your office and in team and board rooms. Make it visible.

Enough reflection! Don't just think about the Improvement Engine and the Physics of Success! Put them into practice. Do it! Start now.

The Improvement Engine is designed to help you change the world. Enjoy the journey…

The Improvement Engine

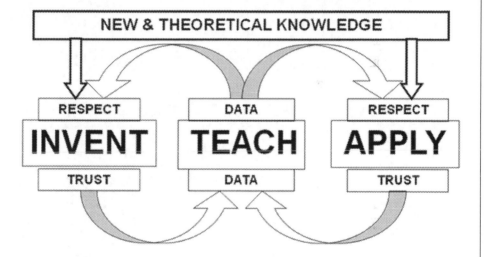